Crochet

patterns · techniques · stitches · inspiration

First published in Great Britain in 2006 by MQ Publications Limited

New edition published in 2010 by Bounty Books,
a division of Octopus Publishing Group Ltd
Reprinted 2012

This edition published in 2013 by Bounty Books,
a division of Octopus Publishing Group Ltd
Endeavour House
189 Shaftesbury Avenue
London WC2H 8JY
Reprinted 2014

www.octopusbooks.co.uk

An Hachette UK Company
www.hachette.co.uk

Copyright © Octopus Publishing Group Ltd 2006

Photography: Lizzie Orme

ISBN: 978-0-753726-60-0

A CIP catalogue record for this book is available from the British Library

Printed and bound in China

Crochet

edited by Katy Bevan

Bounty
BOOKS

Contents

INTRODUCTION

The main attraction of crochet is that it is both quick to pick up for beginners, and fast to make things. Projects in crochet seem to grow quickly, and with only one hook, and one stitch to drop, it is much more portable. If you are making motifs, you don't even have to take the rest of your project around with you, just a small bobbin and hook that would fit in any handbag or commodious pocket.

However portable it may be, the square crocheted motif has become a bit of a cliché – modern crochet design has come a long way from the ubiquitous granny square. Artists and designers are recognizing the versatility of crochet for fashion and interiors. Throws made from multicoloured 'granny' or 'afghan' squares now change hands in boutiques and antique shops for large sums of money.

The humble art of crochet is quite distinctive. The rows are worked in both directions and the loops of thread are attached both to the row below and to the stitch on either side. This is what distinguishes it from a knitted fabric where the loops are attached only to the rows above and below. The final row of knitting, the bound-off edge, is the only place that a crochet chain appears – as there is no further row to attach to, the loops link to each other as in crochet. Tunisian crochet, worked with a long needle, is different again. Alternate rows are knitted or crocheted creating a very dense material that looks more like knitting.

Crochet has been sometimes reviled, occasionally revered. During a period when it is fashionable to eschew the mass-produced products of the high street stores, the handmade is making a revival. Crochet is so easy to learn, and can be as simple or as complicated as you want it to be, lending itself to unique accessories that label the wearer as thinking for themselves.

This book has over thirty patterns from Bee Clinch's brooches that will only take an evening to make, to the more ambitious blankets that will keep your hands busy for some time. The fashion chapter has a simple shrug designed by

Ruth Maddock that will make up quickly, and a more complicated chevron patterned skirt to challenge the more experienced hookster. For homes, the textured cushions are a perfect project to try out some different stitches, while the fluffy coat hangers experiment with a novelty yarn. The hoarders among us will enjoy Susie Johns's rag-rug pattern for using up all those scraps of fabric, while her string bag will save plenty of carrier bags from landfill sites. For children there is Roz Esposito's cute pixie hat and scarf in the softest alpaca, and Carol Chambers's red-cabled suit for a baby. Bee Clinch's slippers introduce the use of colour charts, while Claire Montgomerie's inspired designs for hats, cuffs and collars will keep you looking at your most fashionable.

The step-by-step sections at the start of the book will guide you through the many stages, from turning a row, right through to circular crochet. Even if you have never picked up a hook before, this book will help you through those first stages, right through to tackling a complicated project.

So what are you waiting for? Get hooking.

part
1

ALL ABOUT CROCHET

A BRIEF HISTORY OF CROCHET

Crochet may have had its origins in nalbinding, an ancient form of looped fabric worked on a single pin. Items using this technique have been discovered in ancient Middle Eastern sites from the third century AD and Egyptian tombs of the fourth and fifth centuries AD.

Crochet as we know it today is really a Victorian development. Two pioneering writers on knitting and crochet, Mlle Riego de la Branchardiere and Cornelia Mee (*The Manual of Needlework*, 1845) both claim it as their own invention. An earlier form of crochet, known as shepherd's crook knitting, had been known in the UK since the eighteenth century, but the Victorian exponents dismissed this as 'common' and devised a huge variety of beautiful patterns of their own.

Mlle Riego was awarded the only Gold Medal for crochet at the Great Exhibition of 1851 at the Crystal Palace, London, and is credited with popularizing Irish crochet. At her death she left a great deal of her fortune to help Irish industries. She published several volumes of tatting patterns using what we now think of as picot crochet stitches.

These mid-Victorian publications on knitting and crochet were expensive and aimed at the leisured classes. However, following the 1870s Education Act and the spread of literacy, cheap magazines such as Weldon's 2d series, *Needlecraft* and Leach's 1d editions emerged. At last, every industrious housewife could adorn her home with crochet doilies, counterpanes and antimacassars, and her underclothes with delicate edgings.

Magazines continued to offer a wide variety of crochet patterns well into the 1920s. Marjory Tillotson, working for J & J Baldwin, produced the very first printed leaflet in Britain in 1908. It featured a crochet jacket and cap. She went on to produce delightful booklets for the company such as *The Busy Bee Knitting and Crochet Book* and the very first edition of *Woolcraft* in 1914.

During the 1930s, apart from fine household items, the interest in crochet declined, but in the 1950s a revival took place in America and quickly spread to Europe. Publishers offered excellent books devoted to crochet and by the '70s crochet designs were at the forefront of the catwalk.

Like knitting, crochet has undergone periods of decline and popularity. Happily, thanks to innovative designers like the ones featured in this book, and the availability of beautiful yarns, crochet is back in its rightful place.

Sheila Williams

Opposite and left:
Pattern book covers from the 1940s show that crochet was a popular craft for accessories and homewares. Afghan, or 'granny square' coverlets and throws are just as popular now as they were with the Early American Pioneers.

STAR BOOK No. 70

10 CENTS

Hot Plate Mats

CROCHET
FOR YOUR HOME

BOOK 67
PRICE 10 CENTS

BOOK NO. 271

10¢

Edgings
FOR HANDKERCHIEFS

parade's
CROCHET
COLLECTION

Full Directions
For 24 Items

Fashion · Home · Boutique

COATS & CLARK'S O.N.T.   KITCHEN CROCHET   BOOK No. 304   10¢

Kitchen Crochet
FEATURING "Speed-Cro-Sheen"

BOOK No. 162

PRICE 10 CENTS

EDGINGS

COATS & CLARK'S   FASHIONS IN QUICK CROCHET   BOOK NO. 302   10¢

Fashions
IN
QUICK CROCHET

NEW IDEAS IN "Speed-Cro-Sheen"

COATS & CLARK'S O.N.T.   QUICK TRICKS   BOOK No. 307   10¢

new
QUICK TRICKS
to crochet and knit

COATS   TABLE SETTINGS   BOOK No. 321   10¢

the NEW LOOK in
TABLE SETTINGS

CROCHET IN FASHION

There is only one thing lower than knitting in the craft pantheon, and that is the humble art of crochet. Apparently first recorded in Victorian times, crochet has made various forays into fashion. Crochet has always been popular for making collars and clothing, and embellishing tablecloths and handtowels.

There is no evidence to prove that crochet existed before the 1800s, although it was probably used as a form of lace making. Some techniques, such as 'nun's work' from fourteenth-century Italy, sound as if they may have been an early form of delicate crochet work. Other theories are that it was developed in Arabia, and came to Europe through trade routes. The French lace-embroidery technique of tambouring also used a similar hooking technique.

The first recorded use of crochet patterns, similar to Irish Crochet, indicates they were developed to replace complicated bobbin lace techniques. Crochet is still considered the poor cousin of lace, since it was born out of imitation of this exclusive product. However, this also meant it was a craft without boundaries – a pastime enjoyed by noblewomen and peasants alike.

Pioneers in the new American states crocheted reams of luxurious lace with which to adorn pillowslips and petticoats and in Europe crocheted lace became an affordable luxury for the many.

The new craft didn't make the leap away from doilies and lace mats until it made its way in the 1950s and 1960s from a homemaker's craft in thread and steel pins, to fashionable garments made with thicker yarns. The popular 'granny' or

Left: An early *Coats* pattern from 1965 shows a collar and cuff design in Irish Crochet. These imitation lace patterns were popular to update clothing cheaply.
Right: A fashionable pattern style from 1970 – a crocheted yellow nylon mini-dress complete with patent leather white boots pays homage to the Mary Quant look that was in vogue at the time.

super nylon d.k.

bust 34/36"   15 balls

CROCHET IN

SIRDAR

5051

1/- (5p)

'afghan' square became the basis of countless coverlets. Picked up by the fashion industry, crochet became the handmade form for mini-skirts and dresses.

In 1955 Mary Quant opened Bazaar, a shop on the King's Road, London. Here she sold inexpensive, brightly coloured, simple clothes which were immediate hits with the 16 to 25 year-old market. These included skinny rib jumpers, ready-to-wear mini-skirts and dresses, coloured tights, hipster belts, PVC garments and sleeveless crochet tops and hats. Worn with knee-high patent leather boots, the crochet top was as much a part of the look as the infamous mini-skirt.

Designers as diverse as Jurgen Lehl, Bernard Willhelm, Chanel and Yohji Yamamoto have used crochet in their new season's ranges. Not just the preserve of the autumn lines, crochet dresses and skirts are popular in the summer season too, avoiding the seasonal nature of most knitwear. Jewellery designers are also using crochet with precious metal wires and beads to make beautiful and delicate ornaments.

In the twenty-first century, crochet is gaining fashion credibility. In recent years crochet and knitting have also become an acceptable medium for expression, alongside more traditional media such as watercolour, oil paints and so on. Students in art colleges are using more textile techniques in their work. Crochet is beginning to be accepted as an applied art, rather than a craft purely for domestic use, thus raising its status in the eyes of the world. So the humble granny square and talented young hooksters can now take crochet to new heights of fashion.

Left: Crochet was considered groovy in 1966.
Right: High fashion from the Spring/Summer 2005 catwalk shows from designer Alice Temperley (image courtesy of Catwalking.com).

HOOKS AND EQUIPMENT

Compared to some other crafts, there is very little essential or obscure equipment needed for crochet. Most of the items will already be in your sewing basket. You may even have a hook already, for picking up dropped stiches in knitting or mending. It is really only the hooks which are particular, and it is best to experiment to find the most comfortable for you.

Crochet hooks come in all shapes and sizes. Older hooks were carved from wood, bone or ivory. Some early bakelite and resin hooks can still be found in antique shops, although increasingly sought after.

Labelling of hooks happens in several ways. The modern metric system measures the actual diameter of the hook, so is the most reliable method. However, older hooks from Europe, and hooks from the US have their own labelling system with letters and numbers which can be confusing. You can convert using the chart at the back of this book (page 190) but the recommended method is to use a needle gauge and measure the actual diameter in millimetres.

Fine steel hooks, or pins, are generally used for the finest crochet work with shiny, mercerized cotton or silks and have a different sizing protocol. Chunky and novelty yarns can be worked with giant plastic hooks. Hooks turned in the finest woods are beautiful to handle, although many hooksters prefer the speed of an aluminium hook with a soft and ergonomic gripped rubber handle.

Yarns that can split, will split when you try to crochet with them. Any kind of long thread can be crocheted, however the best results are often obtained with smooth well-spun yarns. Some yarns come in skeins, although they are not so common these days. When this happens you will need to find a willing pair of hands to help, or enlist the back of an upright chair in order to wind the yarn into a usable ball. Always wrap the yarn around several fingers when winding a ball so that the ball remains loose and does not stretch the yarn.

Other equipment

Sharp scissors are needed for cutting yarn and trimming ends. It is best to keep these in your work-basket lest they get used for cutting paper and become blunt.

Blunt needles are great as they don't split the yarn as you are sewing up. Blunt needles that have a large eye are best for those fluffy novelty yarns.

Knitter's pins have large heads for pinning together shapes without disappearing through the holes.

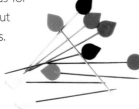

Pincushion's can be used, with at least one blunt-ended or tapestry needle for sewing up seams and threading in ends. The pincusion below is handy as it fits onto your wrist as you are working.

Pom-pom templates are useful if you are making many pom-poms. However, it is simplicity itself to make them out of cardboard. Some templates have removable centres, so that you can alter the size of the pom-pom. Others, like the green ones below come in four pieces. The two halves are wound separately, saving time, and are then put together at the end.

A workbox is a must to keep together all your equipment once you get going. A hook roll is easy to make, and lovely ones are available to purchase. This will let you see at a glance which sizes you have in your collection. You will also need somewhere to keep the inevitable piles of embroidery yarn, buttons and ribbons, all of which are invaluable for embellishing your crochet work.

part

2

CROCHET BASICS

GETTING STARTED

The basics of crochet are very simple. Once you have made a basic chain you are well on your way, as even the most complicated and decorative stitches are just variations on this simple stitch. These instructions are all for a right-handed person. If you are left-handed, look at the step images in a mirror and they should show you the correct way to do the stitch.

Holding the hook and yarn

To crochet successfully it is important to hold the yarn and hook in a correct and comfortable manner. This will ensure that the gauge is accurate and consistent throughout your chosen project. There are many individual ways of holding the hook and yarn in crochet and it may feel awkward at first. Here are just two examples – choose whichever variation seems to come naturally to you.

Holding the hook

Hold the hook in your right hand as you would a knife, controlling the hook with your thumb and forefinger.

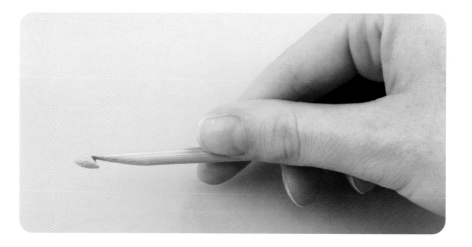

Or, hold the hook in your right hand as you would a pencil. Although elegant, many people find this method cumbersome when working at speed.

Holding the yarn

Wrap the ball end of the yarn around the little finger of your left hand, passing it under the third and middle finger and over the forefinger, using your forefinger to create tension.

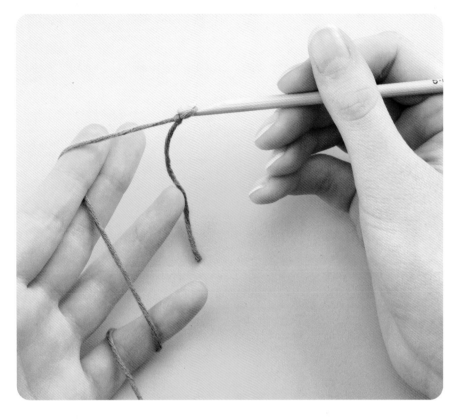

Or, wrap the ball end of the yarn around the little finger of your left hand, passing it over the other three fingers. Hold the work steady with your thumb and forefinger and use the middle finger to create tension.

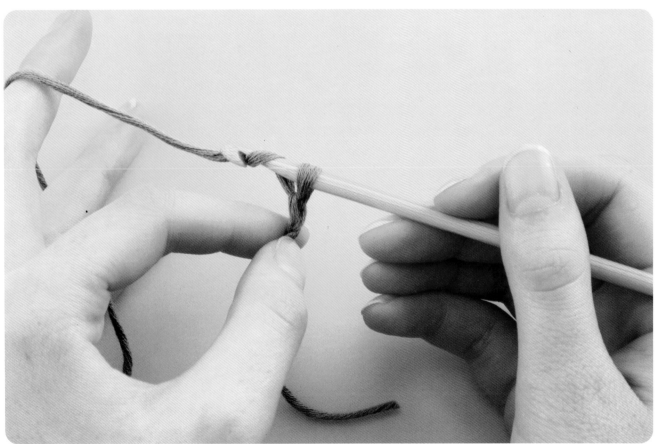

Make a slipknot

1 Make a loop in the yarn. With your crochet hook catch the ball end of the yarn and draw through the loop.

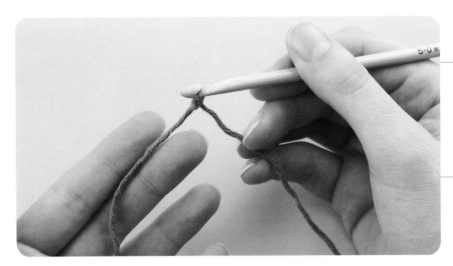

2 Pull firmly on yarn and hook to tighten knot and create the first loop.

Make a chain

1 To make a chain, hold the short tail end of yarn with the left hand and bring the ball end of yarn round hook (yrh) by passing hook in front of the yarn, under and around it.

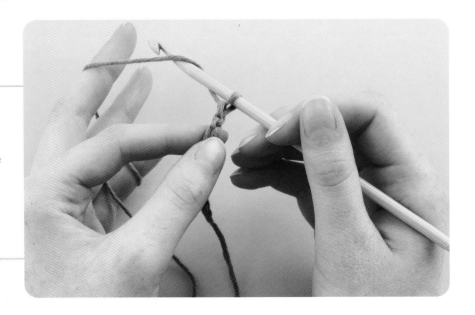

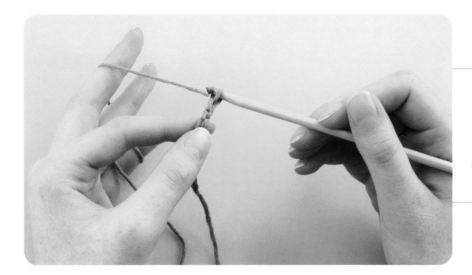

2 Keeping the tension in the yarn taut, draw the hook and yarn through the loop creating a further loop.

3 Begin at step 1 again, and repeat to make the number of chain stitches required, ensuring that the stitches are fairly loose. As the chain lengthens keep hold of the bottom edge to maintain the tension.

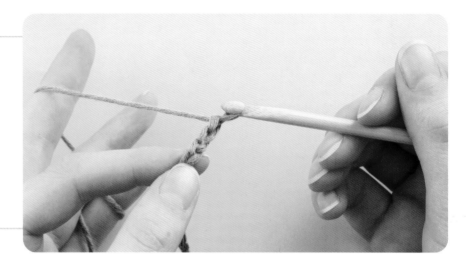

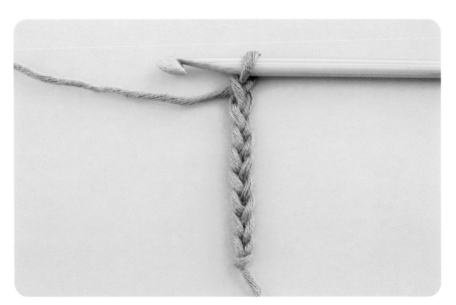

How to count a chain

To count the stitches, use the right side of the chain, or the side that has more visible and less twisted 'V' shapes, as shown in this picture. Don't count the original slip stitch, but count each 'V' as one chain. There are eight stitches on this chain.

Make a slip stitch (sl st)

A slip stitch is used to join one stitch to another or a stitch to another point, as in joining a circle, and is usually made by picking up two strands of a stitch, however, where it is worked into the starting chain only pick up the back loop, as shown here.

1 Insert the hook into the back loop of the next stitch and pass the yarn round the hook (yrh), as in chain stitch.

2 Draw yarn through both loops on stitch and repeat.

Turning a row

At the end of a row, when you turn the work to begin the next, you need to complete a turning chain to get to the right height of the stitch you are working. This chain counts as the first stitch in the row, and each technique, depending on its height, uses a different number of chain stitches at the start of the row.

1 After completing a row, turn work. Make turning chain in the same way as a normal chain; yrh.

2 Draw yarn through loop on hook and repeat to height of chain required (consult table below).

Turning chain table

Type of stitch	No. of chain stitches
double	1
half treble	2
treble	3
double treble	4
triple treble	5

Double crochet (dc)

Here you can see that the hook is passed through the whole stitch (two strands).

1 Insert hook, front to back into next stitch, two strands and one loop on hook; yrh.

2 Draw yarn through to front, two loops on hook.

3 Yrh, keeping the tension with the left hand.

4 Draw yarn through both loops to complete double crochet. Work one dc into every stitch to end.

Half treble crochet (htr)

This is a popular stitch for hats and bags as it makes a firm fabric.

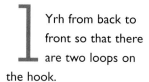 **1** Yrh from back to front so that there are two loops on the hook.

2 Insert hook in next stitch, from front to back; yrh.

3 Draw yarn through so that there are three loops on the hook.

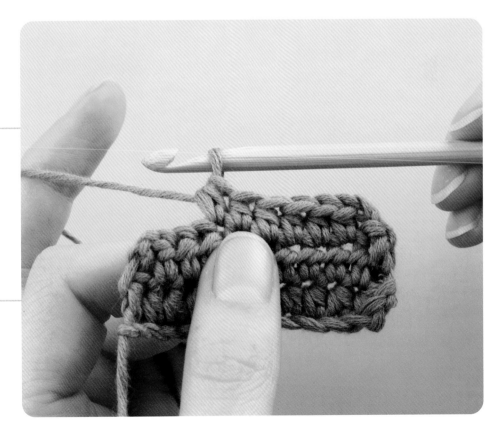

4 Yrh and draw yarn through the three loops on the hook together to complete htr.

Treble crochet (tr)

This makes a more open fabric. The stitch is called a treble in the UK (double in the US) because of the three moves to make the stitch.

1   Yrh from back to front so there are two loops on the hook.

2   Insert hook in next stitch, from front to back; yrh.

3   Draw yarn through, three loops now on hook; yrh.

4 Draw yarn through first two loops, two loops now on hook; yrh.

5 Draw yarn through remaining two loops to complete tr.

Double treble crochet (dtr)

You will need a turning chain of four to reach the height of this elongated stitch.

1 Yrh twice so there are three loops on hook.

2 Insert hook in next stitch, from front to back; yrh.

3 Draw yarn through stitch to front, four loops on hook; yrh.

4 Draw yarn through two loops, leaving three loops on hook; yrh again.

5 Draw yarn through two loops, leaving two loops on hook; yrh.

6 Draw yarn through both remaining loops to complete dtr.

Treble treble crochet (tr tr)

This elongated stitch makes a holey fabric with tall stems.

1 Yrh three times so there are four loops on hook.

2 Insert hook in next stitch, from front to back; yrh.

3 Draw yarn through stitch, five loops now on hook; yrh.

4 Draw yarn through first two loops, four loops now on hook; yrh.

5 Draw yarn through next two loops, three loops now on hook; yrh.

6 Draw yarn through next two loops, two loops now on hook. Yrh and pull through remaining loops to complete tr tr.

WORKING IN THE ROUND

There are two ways to begin circular crochet – with a chain or a loop. The first chain version is easiest to master, but the yarn loop is a useful technique to learn when a hole at the centre of your work would be a problem.

Making a chain ring

1 Work a chain as long as required by pattern. Insert hook in first chain and yrh.

2 Draw yarn through loops on hook to make slip stitch that joins the first chain to the last.

Making a yarn loop

This way of working in the round ensures that there is no hole in the middle of the work, as there is with a chain ring.

1 Make a loop with tail end of yarn on right, ball on left.

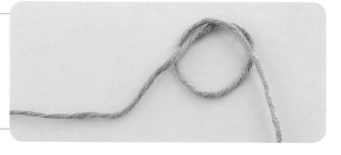

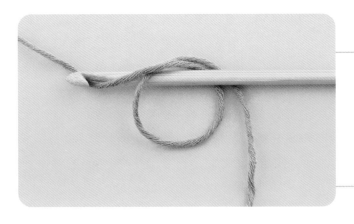

2 Insert hook in loop and wrap the yarn coming from the ball around the hook (you will need to steady work with your hand).

3 Pull yarn through so you have one loop on hook. Yrh and pull through the loop on the hook to make one chain to begin the round.

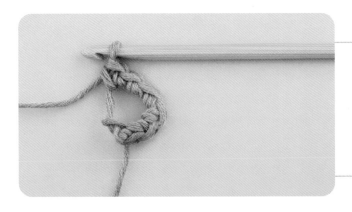

4 Work as many dc, or whatever stitch you are using, into the loop of yarn as required by the pattern.

5 Pull the ends of yarn tight to draw up the circle, so you have no hole left in the middle of the first round.

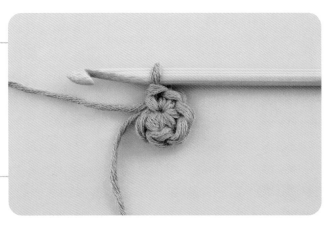

CIRCULAR CROCHET

Working in rounds as opposed to rows means the work continues round and round, with no turning – the last stitch of each round is joined by a slip stitch to the first stitch of that round. This means it is easy to lose which round you are on and stitch markers are a good idea to remind you of where you started. To create a flat circle, rather than a tube, you will need to increase in every row. Work two stitches into each chain in the first round, then every other stitch in the following round, every third stitch in the third round, and so on. At the beginning of each round it is still necessary to make the turning chain (see page 25) even though you are not actually turning the work – unless, however, you are going round in a spiral, which does create a less even shape.

1 To join a new colour, fasten off first colour. Insert hook from front to back in stitch where you wish to begin new colour, and make a slipknot on your hook with the new colour. Draw the hook through to front.

2 Make a turning chain to get work to height of the stitch being used.

3 Insert hook into next stitch and work stitch required by pattern.

4 Continue to work round until you reach the beginning of round, which you may have marked with a stitch marker. Join round with ss to top of first chain.

GRANNY SQUARES

Granny squares are a simple structure to make and can be the basis of many other designs, by joining them together. They can be made in one colour, or in many colours, making them a great way to use up oddments of yarn.

1 Ch 5 and ss in first ch to join ring. Working into ring: ch 3 (counts as first tr) 2tr in ring, *ch 2, 3tr in ring*. Repeat from * to * twice more. Join with sl st to 3-ch at beginning of round. Ch 5 (first 3 are turning chain (1tr), last 2 are 2-ch space).

2 3dc, ch 2, 3dc into first 2-ch space of previous round; this forms corner. *Ch 1, (3dc, ch 2, 3dc) into next 2-ch space.* Repeat from * to * twice more. Join with sl st to 3rd ch of first chain.

3 For next and following rounds: carry on as step 2, using instructions in brackets for corners, then *ch 1, 3dc* into spaces along side of square, with ch 1 before next corner.

Colourful and shapely motifs

Not all motifs have to be square. The cot blanket in this book was made with hexagons (refer to the pattern on page 144 for the full instructions). Once you have the gist of it, you can make any shape or colour that you like.

1 Starting with a 5-ch ring and the first round in white, change to a contrasting colour for the next round. The new colour is attached to the hook with a slipknot before continuing.

2 Break off the yarn leaving a length of about 30 cm for joining the patches together.

Half hexagonal motifs

These are the half-shapes necessary to neaten the edges
of a rectangle made up of hexagons.

1 Work the central chain loop as usual, but then
only half the following round.

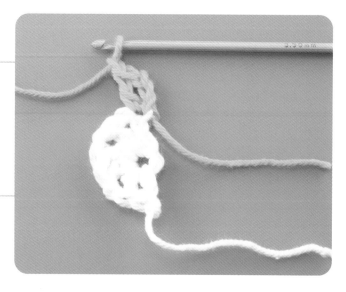

2 Continue working half with the second colour,
creating a straight edge on one side.

3 Finish the final colour and work the edging
as the other shapes, leaving a long end for
sewing up.

Alternative colours

If you are making this cot blanket for a baby yet to be born, you may not know the gender of the baby. You can use neutral colours like yellow and green rather than pink or blue. Afghan motifs are also invaluable for using up oddments, although it is advisable to come up with a general colour scheme, such as shades of blue, and stick to it.

Tip

One of the great things about crochet is that you can carry your work with you and do it on trains, at bus stops and in waiting rooms. If you suddenly have to stop and shove it in your handbag, it doesn't matter: you can easily pick it up again later, where you left off. Unlike knitting, you don't have to worry about lots of stitches falling off needles. A patchwork project is particularly portable because you are only making one patch at a time; once all the patches are made, that is the time to assemble them into the finished item.

Alternative motifs

These further variations on the motif show just how easy it is to make a different kind of square, or even a flower or a star. Just changing the order that the colours are worked can also alter the look.

FINISHING OFF

Finishing is a very important part of crochet as it could make or break your project. The perfect join should be one you can't distinguish from the work, as bad finishing is always noticeable and messy.

Fastening off

1 After finishing the last stitch, snip off the yarn from the ball, leaving about 30 cm to weave in; yrh.

2 Draw all the loose ends of yarn through the final loop and remove the hook. Pull on the yarn to tighten the loop.

Weaving in ends

1 Use the hook to draw the loose yarn through at least five stitches, winding the yarn over and under as you go, to secure yarn and ensure it doesn't work free.

2 Snip off excess yarn close to the work.

Blocking

When you have fastened off and sewn
or woven in all your loose ends, it is
often a good idea to block your work.
This gives you an opportunity to make
sure that any garment pieces are the
right size as specified in your pattern,
and that the edges are neat and even.

Place your work on a soft terry
towel, spray with a fine mist of water
and press lightly with a cloth over the
work. Avoid ironing directly onto the
surface of your work as this will flatten
the texture.

Novelty yarns, and more textured
work may not need blocking. In fact it
may be a bad idea. Check the pattern
and any instructions on the ball band
before proceeding. A gentle spray
and spreading the work out with
your hands may suffice if blocking
is not recommended.

Slip-stitch join

Place two pieces together, right sides
facing. Work a row of slip stitch along
the join, inserting needle through back
loops only of both pieces (the two
loops which touch when placed side
by side).

Double-crochet join

Place two pieces together, right sides facing. Work a row of dc along the edges of the two pieces, going through the whole stitches of both pieces.

Whipstitch

Place two pieces together, right sides facing. Using a blunt-ended needle, join the edges of each piece by working diagonal stitches through the back loops along each edge.

MEASURING TENSION

Before starting on a project, it is advisable that you do a tension swatch to ensure that you are crocheting at the right tension. This enables you to correct any deviances from the working pattern before you begin. The swatch should be just over 10 cm (4 inches) square using the same stitch that is used in the pattern, or as indicated by the instructions. Knitter's pins are useful as the large heads won't disappear through the holes in the fabric.

1 Make the swatch then measure out 10 cm along a row (or 4 inches as shown here). Place a pin at either end.

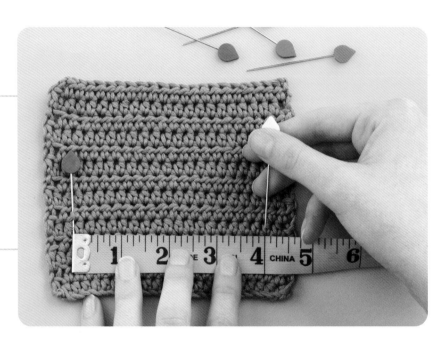

2 Measure out 10 cm (4 inches) across the rows, using pins as markers. Use these two sets of markers to count how many stitches and rows there are to 10 cm (4 inches). Compare this to the tension mentioned at the start of your pattern.

THROUGH BOTH LOOPS?

In early crochet, each stitch would have been worked strictly through the front of the stitch only, creating a significant difference between the texture of the 'right' and 'wrong' sides. These days it is more common to use both strands of the stitch, making the fabric more reversible.

This sample shows the texture created when the hook is pushed through both sides of the stitch.

This sample shows the texture that is made when only the front of the stitch is used.

part

3

BEYOND THE BASICS

SHAPING

Increasing at the beginning of a row

1 Make a length of chain equal to the number of extra stitches required, minus one, plus the number of turning ch required for st being worked. Work across these sts as you would a foundation ch, starting in the ch which will leave the correct turning ch for the st you are using – i.e.: start in the 3rd ch from hook to leave a turning chain 2-ch long.

2 Continue across the row as normal, remembering that the turning chain is now at the beginning of the increased stitches.

At the end of a row

1 At the end of the row, pick up the final stem of the last stitch and make another stitch here.

2 Continue in this way until the required number of stitches have been made. Or, make a chain and turn, working into the chain, then continuing to work along the row.

Increasing in the middle of a row

To increase in middle of a row, work twice into st where increase is required. To create an even increase over several rows: on next row, increase into first of two sts made by previous increase. On following row, increase into second of two sts made by previous increase. Continue to alternate where increase is made in this way until desired number of increases has been completed.

Decreasing at the beginning of a row

To decrease one dc at beginning of row: make one turning ch, skip first st, insert hook into next st and draw loop through, insert hook into next st and draw loop through (3 loops on hook). Yrh and draw through all three loops.

Decreasing at the end of a row

Work across the row until 2dc and turning ch remain. Insert hook in next st; yoh and pull through (3 loops on hook). Insert hook in next st; yrh and pull through all loops on hook.

Decreasing in the middle of a row

Work across to desired position of decrease. Insert hook in next st; yoh and pull through (3 loops on hook). Insert hook in next st; yrh and pull through all loops on hook.

Decreasing in the middle of a row

To create an even decrease over several rows: on next row, start the decrease in st before the decrease on previous row. On following row, start the decrease in st after the decrease on previous row. Continue to alternate where decrease is made in this way until desired number of decreases has been completed.

CHEVRONS

Chevrons are worked horizontally, using increases and decreases to create the zigzag effect. Chevrons look most effective when worked in stripes of colour. This sample is taken from the chevron patterned skirt.

1 To make chevrons, work increases and decreases alternately and at regularly spaced intervals across the row, as in increasing and decreasing in the middle of a row. Then on each following row, work as for the increase and decrease dart, to create the zigzag pattern.

2 In the up angle, increase at the top of the point.

CHANGING COLOUR

To attach a new colour at the beginning or in the middle of a row, work the last stitch of the first colour until two loops remain on the hook, then draw the new colour yarn through these two loops to complete the stitch.

Multiple colours

When the colours of yarn are changed many times in one row, the yarn not in use can be carried along the back of the work, until needed again. However, if areas of colour wider than about 3 or 4 sts are required, a separate ball of yarn should be used for each shape.

On a right side row

On a right side row, yarn is carried along the back. With colour A, work number of stitches required, less one, and work this next stitch leaving the last 2 loops on hook; pick up colour B, carry over A and complete the stitch with B. Using colour B, work number of stitches required, less one, and work this next stitch leaving the last 2 loops on hook; pick up colour A, carry over B and complete the stitch with A. Continue, bringing in whatever colour is required in this way.

On a wrong side row

On a wrong side row, the yarn has to be carried across the front of the fabric. Work number of stitches required for colour A, less one, and work this next stitch leaving the last 2 loops on hook, bring A to the front of the fabric and B to the back, completing the stitch with B. Working with B, work number of stitches required, less one, and work this next stitch leaving the last 2 loops on hook, bring B to the front of the fabric and A to the back, completing the stitch with A. Continue, bringing in whatever colour is required in this way.

BUTTONHOLES

Whether it is for a bag closure, a cardigan or a decorative device, it is often necessary to make buttonholes. Don't be put off as they are not as difficult to master as they may first appear. First you need to decide what kind of purpose the button will serve and then which method is most suitable. The horizontal type is most commonly used, while the vertical buttonhole is better when there will be a lot of strain or tension on the finished make. Then there are loops, which are perhaps more decorative.

Horizontal buttonhole

Work across row until reaching the desired place for buttonhole. Make length of chain, same width as buttonhole. Miss same amount of sts along row as amount of ch, work into next st and continue to next buttonhole position or end of row.

Vertical buttonhole

1 Work across row until reaching the desired place for buttonhole. Turn work and work back and forth on these stitches until desired length of hole has been achieved. Fasten off yarn.

2 Attach yarn to opposite unworked edge of piece. Work up to 1 st from edge of buttonhole, turn and work back and forth on these sts until work measures same as other side. Work across these sts, work 1 chain, then work across sts on other side. Continue to next buttonhole position.

Looped buttonhole

1 Work across row to where desired loop will end and work length of ch to produce right size of loop. Working left to right, attach end of loop with sl st to row being worked, the required number of sts away from beginning of ch (here, 2 sts).

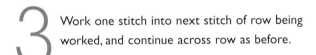

2 Working again from right to left, work same amount of dc as chain into the loop made.

3 Work one stitch into next stitch of row being worked, and continue across row as before.

Making a button

Make a chain of 2 and link together in a ring with a slip stitch. Work 6dc in the ring. Make a turning chain, then make two dc in every st. Increase every other stitch on the next round, then skip every other stitch on the following round to bring the shape in again. Skip every alternate stitch again, then cut the yarn, pull it through the last loop and draw up tightly. Stuff the ends of the yarn inside, using the long end to sew in place.

CLUSTER STITCHES

These are made up of groups of stitches that are only half finished, worked into the same space, and then joined together. The number of stitches worked will vary between stitches and patterns but the result is an interesting texture that increases surface interest.

Bobbles

When working this stitch on every row put at least one treble stitch between each bobble. You can also experiment by varying how many tr you work into the same space. The stitch is worked from the wrong side, so you don't see the bobbles until you turn the work around.

1   To make 1 bobble: *yrh, insert hook into st, yrh, draw a loop through, yrh, draw through 2 loops. Repeat from * 4 more times, inserting hook in same st each time, so there are 6 loops on hook; yrh.

2   Draw the yarn through all loops on hook to complete one bobble. The bobble will have a raised, spherical look on the side of work facing away from you.

Popcorns

These are a variation on the basic bobble where the shapes are more irregular and slant from side to side.

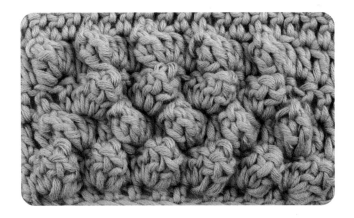

1 Work 1tr, then work five tr into the next stitch.

Tip

If you want the popcorn to slant in the opposite direction, work step 1, then in step 2, insert the needle from back to front before completing the stitch.

2 Remove hook from working loop. Insert from front to back into top of first tr in the group, then back through working loop. Yrh, draw through all loops to complete one popcorn.

Puffs

The texture of puffs is similar to bobbles and popcorns, but slightly less pronounced. Experiment by varying how many loops you work into same space while keeping one treble between each puff.

1 *Yrh, insert in st, yrh and draw loop through loosely. Repeat from * 5 more times into same st (13 loops on hook).

2 Yrh and pull through 12 loops – 2 loops on hook. Yrh and pull through remaining loops to complete one puff st.

Shell patterns

A combination of shells and filet chains make an open sample (right) while a simple shell pattern (far right) makes a firmer, more closed fabric.

Shells

These scalloped patterns have the added advantage of creating a pretty edge to your work. Alternate the shell clusters with double crochet along a row. To create the half-drop shell repeat in this picture, begin the first row with a dc and the second with a shell cluster, repeating the two rows throughout.

1 Work five dc into next st – one shell cluster made.

2 Work one dc into following st, then work one shell cluster into next st. Continue in this way along the row.

Shells and blocks are alternated to make an all-over lacy pattern (far right) while the pattern near right has the shells directly above each other, rather than brick style as shown in the steps above.

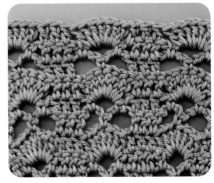

FILET CROCHET

'Filet' literally means 'net', and filet crochet is a net or mesh, where blocks can be filled in to form shapes. Filet crochet is made up of chains and trebles. Trebles worked in groups form the blocks and chains the spaces. Patterns are usually worked from a chart.

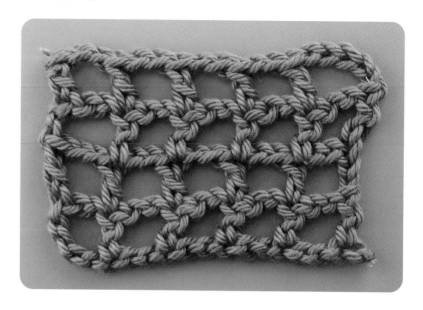

Basic filet

To make the basic filet mesh, make a length of chain with multiples of 3 plus 1. Ch 4 then work 1tr into 8th ch from hook – this 7ch forms a 2-ch space along the bottom edge, a 3-ch to count as first tr, and a 2-ch space on row being worked. *1tr into next ch, ch 2, skip 2ch. Repeat from * along row to end, 1tr in last st; turn.

Lace patterns

This lacy shell pattern is used in the collar pattern later in the book. These arches (far right) are worked in simple chains and trebles to achieve a regular spaced pattern.

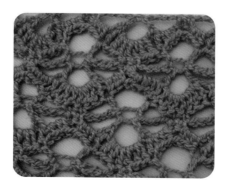

Making blocks in filet

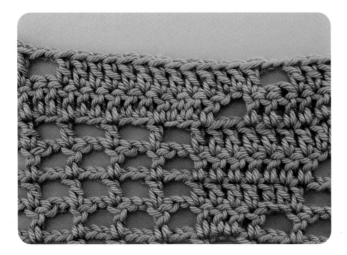

To make patterns in filet work, you can create shapes made up of blocks of treble sts. Stop alternating between blocks of tr and chain spaces, and work tr across the row until you've made a block the required size. Put in chain spaces as required.

Ch 5 (counts as first tr and 1 ch sp), skip first tr, 1 tr into next tr, *ch 2, skip 2-ch, 1 tr into next tr. Repeat from * along row, working last tr into 5th ch of 7-ch at beginning of previous row; turn. These 2 rows form pattern.

To make a mesh with blocks 4 sts wide, where the first row starts with a block: make a ch in multiple of 3 plus 1. Ch 3 (counts as first tr), 1 tr into 4th ch from hook, then 1 tr into each of next 2ch.

The blockwork, right, is a large open pattern of blocks within a frame. The trellis (far right) is a lacy openwork pattern that is not to hard to achieve.

EDGINGS

One of the best ways to employ crochet is in producing neat and even decorative edgings. These edgings need not necessarily be restricted to crochet fabrics; they look just as interesting on knitting or loosely woven fabrics.

Reverse double crochet or corded edging

Join yarn to edge of work. Begin by working one row of dc evenly along the edge of work, being careful not to pull the work too tightly. Then work back along the row in dc, without turning work, from left to right.

Shell edging

Join yarn to edge of work. Begin by working one row of dc evenly along the edge of work, being careful not to pull the work too tightly; turn. Then work a slip stitch into first stitch. *Skip 2 sts, 5tr into next st, skip 2 sts, ss into next st. Repeat from * along length of edge.

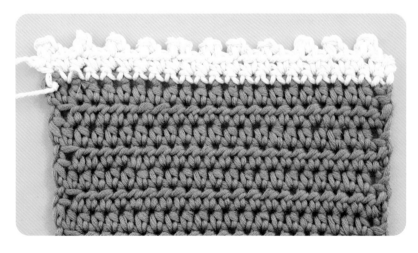

Picot edging

Use either with or without a foundation row of dc (picture shows with foundation row). Then, work 1dc into each of first 3 sts. *Ch 4 then remove hook from last ch and insert in first of 4-ch, pick up chain just dropped and draw through loop on hook to create picot, 1dc into each of next 3 sts. Repeat from * to end.

Triangulation

This deep border is made up of half-afghan squares worked along a straight edge.

Daisy edging

A pretty edging for the more experienced worker.

Ruffle border

Simple edging worked in chains, suitable for the edges of knitting or crochet patterns.

Alternative shell edging

A simple shell-like border for embellishing knitting or crochet alike.

TUNISIAN CROCHET

Tunisian crochet is almost like a mixture of knitting and crochet. It is worked, like crochet on a single hook, but the hook is long enough to build up loops on it, like knitting. You also always work with the right side of the fabric facing you. First, loops are built up on the needle from right to left, then reduced down to one again by working left to right. The row is not fully finished until both of these actions have been completed. Bearing this in mind, the second row is actually a completion of the first. Always remember to work Tunisian crochet loosely as it has a tendency to produce a biased fabric with the edges slanted.

Basic Tunisian stitch

1 Start by making a length of chain that will give the amount of stitches required for your project.
Row 1: insert hook in 2nd ch from hook, yrh, draw loop though and keep this loop on the hook. *Insert hook into next ch, yrh, draw loop though and keep this loop on the hook. Repeat from * to end; do not turn.

2 Row 2: working from left to right, yrh and draw a loop loosely through the first loop on hook, *yrh and draw through next 2 loops on hook. Repeat from * to end, until only working loop remains on hook; do not turn.

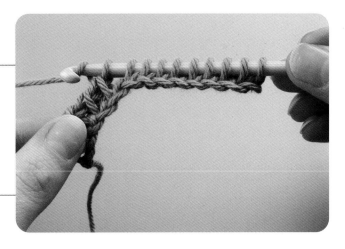

3 Row 3: working from right to left, skip first vertical loop on front of fabric then *insert hook from right to left under vertical loop of next st, yrh, draw loop through, keeping loop on hook, repeat from * to end; do not turn. Row 4 is worked as row 2 and rows 3 and 4 form the pattern, always ending with a row 4.

Tunisian treble stitch

1 Make length of ch which will give amount of sts required.
Row 1: yrh, insert hook into 2nd ch from hook, yrh and draw loop through, yrh and draw a loop loosely through first 2 loops on hook. *Yrh, insert hook into next ch, yrh and draw loop through, yrh and draw loop through first 2 loops. Repeat from * to end; do not turn.

2 Row 2: working from left to right, yrh and draw a loop loosely through the first loop on hook, *yrh and draw through next 2 loops on hook. Repeat from * to end, until only working loop remains on hook; do not turn.

3 Row 3: working from right to left, ch 1 (counts as first st), skip first vertical loop on front of fabric, *yrh, insert the hook from right to left under the vertical loop of next st, yrh and draw a loop through, yrh and draw through 2 loops on hook, repeat from * to end; do not turn. Row 4 is worked as row 2 and rows 3 and 4 form the pattern, always ending with a row 4.

Tunisian stocking stitch

This stitch is so called because it closely resembles stocking stitch in knitting.

1 Make a length of chain that will give the amount of sts required.
Rows 1 and 2: as for the first two rows of basic Tunisian stitch (page 67).
Row 3: working from right to left, *insert hook from front to back, between the verticals of the next st, yrh.

2 Draw the yarn through and keep this loop on hook. Repeat from * in step 1 to the end.
Row 4: as 2nd row of basic Tunisian stitch.
Rows 3 and 4 form the pattern.

Tunisian brick stitch

This stitch is a variation of the basic Tunisian stitch that uses two colours. This sample is begun with a length of ch that's a multiple of 4 sts plus 1.

SPECIAL EFFECTS

There are myriad ways to embellish the surface of your crochet after you have finished.
This could be a final flourish, or an integral part of the design.

Embroidery

Embroidery is an effective way of adding interest to your projects and complements the texture of crochet. Here are some simple stitches that you may like to try. It may help to use a blunt-ended, knitter's needle, as this will not split the yarn as embroidery needles do, and will slip through the crochet stitches easily.

Chain stitch

Insert needle from back to front of work then insert back into same hole, from front to back, to make a loop of thread. Bring needle back to the front through the next hole along, catching up the loop with the needle. Pull the thread through to make first chain. Insert needle from back to front through first chain to make loop for second stitch. This is useful for curved shapes like flowers, or for handwriting.

Blanket stitch

This stitch creates a neat edge, and is useful for straightening an uneven selvedge. Working along the edge, secure yarn at the back of work, insert the needle from front to back, with needle coming out of work over top of loop made by yarn. Pull needle through, tightening yarn against edge of work, repeat along edge.

Satin stitch

Work long straight stitches closely together over the shape you wish to make, keeping edges of the shape even. This is most commonly used as a colour filler for petals and other solid shapes.

Surface crochet

With surface crochet, you can work flat stitches along the surface of a fabric, to create patterns. To work a slip-stitch surface crochet, insert the hook from the front to back of work, yrh at back of fabric, draw loop through to front, *insert hook into next row to be worked, yrh, draw loop through and through loop on hook, rep from * until surface crochet reaches desired length.

Surface edgings

A line of slip stitches is the basis for the shelled edging on the cuffs. This doesn't have to be along a seam, although it can be used to conceal one, but can be anywhere in the body or the edge of the crochet. Make a surface chain as before, then use this as the base for an edging design.

Weaving

This is a splendid way to add not just decoration, but also texture and solidity to a crochet fabric.

Weaving for shape

This close-up of the blue camisole shows how the woven tie adds shape to the garment. Threading is easy with a lacy fabric, or holes can be made specifically for the purpose.

Weaving for effect

Woven effect fabrics can be created by threading yarn through the finished fabric. Simple filet bases are perfect for this. Thread yarn under and over the chain spaces.

Weaving with ribbon

In more densely crocheted fabrics, weaving can be achieved by threading yarn, ribbon or strips of other material over and under the spaces in between stitches.

Tassel border

A fringe or tasselled border is a great way to finish a scarf, or even the edge of a shawl or sweater.

1 Wrap yarn around a rectangle of card until required number of lengths are completed. Cut through loops along one edge of card.

2 With the wrong side of the edge to be fringed facing you, insert a crochet hook through the edge from back to front, hook the folded end of tassel strands onto the hook and pull halfway through fabric. Then insert hook through loop in tassel strands and draw ends through. Pull the knot up tightly. Repeat this action at regular intervals along edge.

Curlicue tassels

To ring the changes, you can make individual curlicues and attach them to the edging. These are created by increasing rapidly. Make a chain the length you want the core to be, say 4–6 cm. On the next row, make 2 stitches into every space (double crochet is fine). To make the curl wider, you can carry on, doubling the number of stitches in each row.

Big tassels

These extra-large tassels are used for the pink shawl. You can tailor them to any project, but the chunkier the yarn, the larger the result.

1 Cut a piece of cardboard 12 x 20 cm. Wrap the yarn loosely round and round the cardboard.

2 Thread a strand through the top and tie firmly leaving a short end and a long end to wind and sew later.

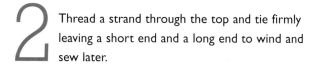

3 Cut through the strands at the bottom of the card with a sharp pair of scissors and trim to even up.

4 Hide the knot and short end at the top under the folded strands. Wind the long end around the top of the tassel a few times and thread it through so it comes out at the top. Use the long end to attach the tassel to your work.

Pom-poms

These fluffy follies are often used on their own, but large clusters of them can be very effective. Use ready-made templates, or make your own.

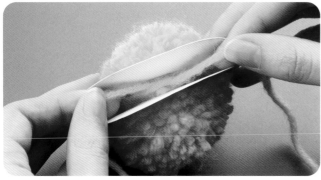

1 Cut out two cardboard circles as big as you want your pom-pom to be. Cut a hole in the centre of each one. Wrap the yarn around the card rings until the hole is full. You can use several strands together. Don't worry if the yarn keeps running out, just leave the ends dangling on the outside.

2 Cut though the yarn at edge until you reach the cardboard. Push the blade of the scissors between the two pieces of card and continue cutting round the edge.

3 Pull the cards apart a little way; wrap a length of yarn around the pom-pom several times, between the pieces of card. Knot firmly but leave the two ends of thread long to sew the pom-pom onto your crocheted piece later.

4 Remove the cards, fluff the pom-pom, and trim with sharp scissors. Different effects can be achieved by altering the yarn. Wrap different colours together for a speckled effect; or one after the other for stripes; and in blocks for a random effect.

part 4

CROCHET HOME

rag-rug bathmat

Any fabrics can be used for this – and it is a great way of recycling old clothes or materials left over from other projects – but the best fabrics to work with are slightly stretchy ones, such as jersey and stockinette, and particularly the type of fabric used to make leotards and opaque tights.

Making the fabric strips

Before you begin, you need to cut your fabric into thin strips, between 6 and 12 mm wide. The width of strips depends on the weight of the fabric – if your chosen material is thin and stretchy, then cut wider strips. If you use the same fabric throughout and cut the strips very accurately, so they are of uniform width, the resulting rug will be quite flat and even with straight edges. But if you vary the fabrics, your rug will have more texture and visual interest and a more uneven finish. Don't reject a fabric just because you don't like the pattern; when cut into strips and crocheted, it will take on an entirely different character.

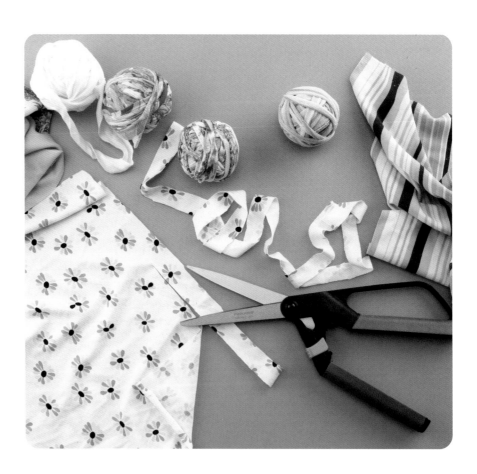

Method

Cut your fabric into strips and, starting with a long strip, ch 50, turn.

Row 1: Ch 1 (counts as first dc), dc to end. Rep row 1 until the work measures 90 cm. When you've used up one strip of fabric, change to the next strip just as you would when changing to a new ball of yarn. Knot the ends of fabric strips together and work in the ends as you go. The knots add to the overall texture of the finished rug.

Tip

Experiment with different colour combinations, such as earthy browns or shades of blue; or combine clashing colours for an eye-catching effect. You can also experiment with texture; try introducing strips of velvet or bouclé fabrics, oddments of textured yarns and even strips cut from plastic bags.

boudoir coat hangers

This is an adults-only version of the children's padded coat hanger. This super fluffy yarn gives the hanger's cover a luxurious finish suitable for the most delicate lingerie.

Coat hanger cover

Measure the width of the hanger and double this measurement. Using col A and 5 mm hook, make a chain to this measurement (approx 16 ch), turn.

Row 1: Ch 1, 1dc into 2nd ch from hook, dc to end, turn.

Cont working in dc until the work, when slightly stretched, is the same length as the hanger, fasten off.

Cover hanger with cotton wadding and trim. Fold the hanger cover in half widthways and mark the centre point of the work with a short length of contrasting yarn. Find the centre point of one short end and join in col A at this point. Fold the hanger cover in half lengthways and then dc the edges together along the short end and down the long edge to about half way. Fit the cover over one end of the coat hanger, passing the hanger's hook between two stitches at the point marked by the contrasting yarn. Dc the edges together until the seam is closed. Fasten off and work the loose end into the hanger.

Flower

Using col B and 4 mm hook, and leaving a reasonable length of yarn at the start of the foundation ch, ch 29, turn.

Row 1: 1tr in 3rd ch from hook, *ch 1, sk 1 ch sp, 1tr, rep from * to end, turn.

Row 2: Ch 2, 1tr, *1tr, 1dtr, 1tr in next ch sp, 1dc in next ch sp, rep from * to last ch sp, 1tr, 1dtr, 1tr in last ch sp, sl st to top of 3-ch, fasten off.

Row 3: Using a 3 mm hook join in col C, ch 2, 1 tr in first st, *2 tr into next st, rep from * to end, fasten off.

Making up

Wind col B around the hanger's hook, starting at the bottom, then working up to the top and back down again. Tie the ends of the yarn together tightly and weave these loose ends into the cover. Thread the loose yarn at the beginning of the flower onto a tapestry needle. Use the needle to work the yarn in and out of the foundation chain. Pull on the end of the yarn to draw the work up and gather it into a flower shape. Fasten off the end and leave yarn. Thread a sewing needle with sewing thread and stitch a vintage button to the centre of the flower. Use the loose end of yarn to stitch the flower at the base of the hanger hook.

YOU WILL NEED:

- GGH Gracia 80% Polyamide, 20% Rayon (90 m per 50 g ball), 1 x 50 g ball in lilac 16 or pink 15 (col A)
- Approximately 25 g of black Aran yarn for flower and hanger hook (col B)
- Small amount 4-ply yarn for flower trim (col C)
- Wooden coat hanger (any size, according to preference)
- Cotton wadding to cover hanger
- Vintage button
- 5 mm, 4 mm and 3 mm hooks
- Tapestry needle
- Sewing needle and thread to match the button

Note

Yarn amounts are based on average requirements and are approximate.

Tension

Not crucial as yarn is elasticated.

textured cushions

This Aran weight yarn is a luxurious blend of merino wool and cashmere that makes up these covers quickly. Make both sides of the cushion in pattern, or use a plain stitch for the back, or even use a matching fabric on the back for a contrast.

Cream ribbed cushion

The front of this cushion is thickly textured; the back is worked in double crochet, to speed things up and to save yarn. If you want to work the whole cushion in the ribbed pattern, you will need 16 balls instead of 12.

Using col A and 3.5 mm hook, ch 81, turn.
Row 1: 1dc in 2nd ch from hook, dc to end (80 sts), turn.
Cont in rows of dc until work measures 26 cm; this forms one part of the back of the cushion.
To work the front of the cushion: Change to 4 mm hook and work in pattern as follows.
Row 1: Ch 3 (counts as first tr), tr to end (80 sts), turn.
Row 2: Ch 2, then work in rftr (ie. work tr sts into the stems of the sts on prev row, inserting hook from right to left, on the front of the work) to end, turn.
Rep row 2 until work measures 76 cm.
To work the other part of the back, change to 3.5 mm hook and cont in rows of dc until work measures 110 cm.
Buttonholes
Next row: Ch 1, 12dc, (ch 3, sk 3 sts, 14dc) 3 times, ch 3, sk 3 sts, 13dc, turn.
Next row: Ch 1, dc to end, fasten off.

YOU WILL NEED:

- Debbie Bliss Cashmerino Aran, 53% merino, 33% microfibre, 12% cashmere (90 m per 50 g ball)

Cream ribbed cushion
- 12 x 50 g balls in cream 101 (col A)
- 50 cm x 50 cm cushion pad

Pink diagonal pattern cushion
- 9 x 50 g balls in dusty pink 602 (col B)
- 60 cm x 40 cm cushion pad

Moss-stitch cushion
- 9 x 50g in pale pink 603 (col C)
- 40 cm x 40 cm cushion pad
- 4 mm and 3.5 mm hooks
- Buttons – 4 for each cushion
- Tapestry needle

Tension
Moss-stitch: 15 sts and 11 rows to 10 cm. Diagonal: 19 st and 10 rows to 10 cm. Ribbed: 18 sts and 7.5 rows to 10 cm.

Making up
Fold up the back parts of the cushion, RS together, so that the short edges overlap (the buttonhole edges should be underneath). Using a tapestry needle and length of matching yarn, sew up the side seams of the cushion. Turn to the RS. Mark the positions of the buttons and stitch in place. Insert the pad and close the cushion with the buttons.

Pink diagonal pattern cushion

This cushion is patterned all over. The pattern seems challenging at first, when you see it written down, but it is easy to master and relatively simple and quick to do, resulting in an attractive pattern of raised horizontal and diagonal lines.

Using col B and 4 mm hook, ch 75, turn.

Row 1: 1 dc into 2nd ch from hook, dc to end (74 sts), turn.

Row 2: Ch 3, *sk next st, 3tr, yrh, insert hook into skipped stitch from back to front, and work 1tr (which crosses diagonally over 3tr just worked), rep from * to end, turn.

Row 3: Ch 1, dc to end, turn.

Rows 2 and 3 form patt, continue working these two rows until work measures 130 cm.

Buttonholes

Next row: Ch 1, (12dc, ch 3, sk 3 sts) 4 times, 13dc.

Next row: Ch 1, dc to end, fasten off.

Making up

Overlap the short edges by 10 cm so the buttonhole edge is underneath and the WS of the work is facing out. Pin along the sides of the overlap. Lay the cushion flat so that the overlap is centred and then pin the sides of the cushion together. Using a tapestry needle and length of matching yarn, sew up the side seams. Turn to the RS. Mark the positions of the buttons and stitch in place. Insert the pad and close the cushion with the buttons.

Moss-stitch cushion

This cushion is patterned all over. The pattern is easy to do, even for a novice, and produces a soft, subtle texture.

Using col C and 4 mm hook, ch 68, turn.

Row 1: 1htr in front lp of 3rd ch from hook, *1htr in back lp of next st, 1htr in front lp of next st, rep from * to end, turn.

Rep this row until work measures 90 cm.

Buttonholes

Next row: Ch 1, 11dc, (ch 3, sk 3 sts, 10dc) 4 times, turn.

Next row: Ch 1, dc to end, fasten off.

curtain tiebacks

These floral tiebacks are both useful and beautiful. Dahlias, chrysanthemums and daisies are here hooked in hothouse colours. Make yours to match your curtains.

Band (make 2 alike)

Using col B, ch 121, turn.

Row 1: 1dc in 3rd ch from hook, dc to end, turn.

Row 2: Ch 2 (counts as 1dc), dc to end (120 sts), turn.

Rep last row 6 more times (8 rows), fasten off.

Hanging loop

Rejoin yarn at one corner of band. Work 2 sl st along narrow edge of band (each st is the depth of a row), ch 6, skip 4 rows, 2 sl st over rem 2 rows, fasten off. Rep at other end of band then rep on 2nd band.

Leaf (make 8 alike)

Using col D, ch 10, turn.

Row 1: 1dc in 2nd ch from hook, 1htr, 1tr, 2dtr, 1tr, 1htr, 1dc, 1 sl st, ch 1, turn.

Row 2: Working along the other side of foundation ch, 1 sl st, 1dc, 1htr, 1tr, 2dtr, 1tr, 1htr, 2dc, fasten off.

Dahlia (make 4 alike)

Using col D, ch 3.

Rnd 1: (RS) 6 dc in first ch of foundation ch, sl st to 3rd ch of foundation ch (7 sts – first 2-ch of foundation ch counts as 1dc).

Rnd 2: (RS) Ch 3, *1dc in next dc, ch 1, rep from * 6 times, sl st to 2nd of 3-ch at beg of rnd (7 ch sp), fasten off.

Rnd 3: (RS) Join in col A at beg of any ch sp, [1 sl st, ch 2, 2tr, ch 2, 1 sl st] into each ch sp (7 petals), turn.

Rnd 4: (WS) Working behind this last rnd of petals, work into each of the 7 dc of 2nd rnd; ch 4 (counts as 1dc and 2 ch), *1dc into next dc, ch 2, rep from * 5 times more, sl st to 2nd of 4-ch at beg of rnd (7 ch sp), turn.

Rnd 5: (RS) [1 sl st, ch 3, 2dtr, ch 3, 1 sl st] into each ch sp (7 petals), turn.

Rnd 6: (WS) Working behind this last rnd of petals, work into each of the 7 dc of 4th rnd; ch 5 (counts as 1dc and 3 ch), *1dc into next dc, ch 3, rep from * 5 times more, sl st to 2nd of 5-ch at beg of rnd (7 ch sp), turn.

Rnd 7: (RS) Join in col C at beg of any ch sp, [1 sl st, ch 3, 3dtr, ch 3, 1 sl st] into each ch sp (7 petals), turn.

Rnd 8: (WS) Working behind this last rnd of petals, work into each of the 7 dc of 6th rnd; ch 6 (counts as 1dc and 4 ch), *1dc into next dc, ch 4, rep from * 5 times more, sl st to 2nd of 6-ch at beg of rnd (7 ch sp), turn.

YOU WILL NEED:

- Patons 100% Cotton DK, mercerized cotton (210 m per 100 g ball), 1 x 100 g ball each of Azalea 02718 (col A), Pansy 02707 (col B), Foxglove 02706 (col C), and Peacock 02705 (col D)
- 1 skein orange stranded cotton
- 3.5 mm crochet hook
- Embroidery needle
- Tapestry needle

Tension
20 dc and 24 rows = 10 cm.

Finished measurements
Length is 60 cm.

Rnd 9: (RS) [1 sl st, ch 3, 2dtr, ch 3, 1 sl st, ch 3, 2dtr, ch 3, 1 sl st] in each ch sp (14 petals), fasten off.

Daisy (make 2 alike)

Using col D, ch 3.

Rnd 1: 7dc in first ch of foundation ch, sl st to 3rd ch of foundation ch (8 sts – first 2 ch of foundation ch counts as 1dc).

Rnd 2: Ch 2 (tc), 1dc in base of tc, 2dc into each dc of prev rnd working into back lp only of each st, sl st to 2nd ch of tc (16 dc – tc counts as 1 dc).

Rnd 3: Join in col B with a sl st to any dc of 2nd rnd, working into back lp only, ch 9, sl st back into same st, *sl st into next st, working into back loop only, ch 9, sl st back into same st, rep from * into each dc of 2nd rnd (16 ch lps).

Rnd 4: Sl st into front lp of dc from 2nd rnd where joined in col B, ch 7, sl st back into same st, *sl st, into next dc from 2nd rnd, working into front lp only, ch 7, sl st back into same st, rep from * into front lp of each dc of 2nd rnd (16 ch lps), fasten off.

Michaelmas Daisy (make 4 alike)

Using col D, ch 3.

Rnd 1: 7dc in first ch of foundation ch, sl st to 3rd ch of foundation ch (8 sts – first 2 ch of foundation ch counts as 1dc), fasten off.

Rnd 2: Join in col B with a sl st to any dc of first rnd, working into back lp only, ch 8, sl st back into same st, *sl st, into next st, working into back lp only, ch 8, sl st back into same st, rep from * into each dc of first rnd (8 ch lps).

Rnd 3: Sl st into front lp of dc from first rnd where joined in col B, ch 6, sl st back into same st, * sl st, into next dc from first rnd, working into front lp only, ch 6, sl st back into same st, rep from * into front lp of each dc of first rnd (8 ch lps), fasten off.

Chrysanthemum (make 2 alike)

Using col D, ch 3.

Rnd 1: 5dc in first ch of foundation ch, sl st to 3rd ch of foundation ch (6 sts – first 2 ch of ch counts as 1dc).

Rnd 2: Ch 2 (tc), 1 dc in base of tc, 2dc into each dc of prev rnd working into back lp only of each st, sl st to 2nd ch of tc (12 dc – tc counts as 1 dc), fasten off.

Rnd 3: Join in col A with a sl st to any dc of 2nd rnd, working into back lp only; *ch 8, 1dc into 3rd ch from hook, 1dc into each of rem 5 ch, sl st in back lp of next dc on 2nd rnd, rep from * all rnd, working last sl st into front lp of dc on 2nd rnd where joined in col B (12 petals).

Rnd 4: Working into front lps only of dc on 2nd rnd; *ch 7, 1dc in 3rd ch from hook, 1dc into each of rem 4 ch, sl st in front lp of next dc of 2nd rnd, rep from * all rnd, working last sl st into first sl st of rnd (12 inner petals), fasten off.

Rnd 5: Join in col C with a sl st into front lp only of any st on first rnd; *ch 6, sl st back into same st, ch 6, sl st to next st, rep from * all rnd (12 ch lps) fasten off.

Finishing off

Weave in all yarn ends and secure; trim off any excess yarn. Thread an embroidery needle with some of the stranded cotton and work a circle of chain sts around the centre of each dahlia. Work chain stitch in the centre loops of each chrysanthemum. On the Michaelmas daisy, make 6 long stitches around the centre of the flower, radiating out from the centre point. Work a large French knot at the centre of each of the daisies. Lightly steam each of the flowers and arrange the petals. do not press. Leave to dry.

Making up

Take each band and thread a tapestry needle with yarn in a contrasting colour. Use this to mark the point 30 sts in from one end and 4 rows up from the long edge on each band. This marks the centre of the floral motif. Fold one band in half widthways and lay out, with the fold to the left. Arrange half of the flowers and leaves around the point marked with the thread using the photograph as a guide. Sew in place and repeat with the remaining band but lay out with the fold to the right, reversing the positioning.

linen sheet edgings

Natural undyed cotton or linen thread beautifully complements a natural colour scheme for a vintage look. This edging can be made as long or short as you like so you can adapt it to decorate sheets and pillowcases of any dimension.

The edging is made widthways. In other words, you don't have to start by making a foundation chain to the desired finished length, you simply work the edging until it is as long as you need it. Before you begin, make a short length of about 10 pattern repeats complete with scalloped and straight edges, and then measure this and use it as a guide to work out how many pattern repeats will fit along the edge of your sheet.

Method

Using 2 mm hook, ch 9, turn.

Row 1: 1tr in 8th ch from hook, ch 2, 1tr in same ch, ch 2, (1tr, ch 2, 1tr) in last ch, turn.

Row 2: Ch 5, 1tr into 2-ch sp, (ch 2, 1tr) 3 times in same sp, turn.

Rep row 2 until you have worked the desired number of repeats, do not turn.

To work the straight edge:

Next row: (Worked back along the length of the edging) *ch 4, 2dc in next 5-ch lp, rep from * to end, finishing with 2dc into ch lp on first row, fasten off.

To work the scalloped edge:

Next row: Rejoin the yarn to the last 5-ch lp at other end of the edging, ch 3, 8tr into this ch sp, *9tr into next 5-ch loop, rep from * to end, finish with a sl st into ch lp on first row, fasten off.

Tip

Most crochet patterns, traditional or modern, combine only a few very basic stitches: chain, slip stitch and double crochet (or variants of double crochet such as treble, half treble, double treble and so on). Once you have mastered these few stitches – and they really are very easy – you can attempt quite complex patterns. This edging is actually very easy to do and can be made up in other yarns, if you prefer. For example, use a thicker gauge of cotton thread (and a correspondingly larger hook) to make an edging for a towel; or try using a soft, fluffy yarn to make a border for a cardigan or jacket.

trinket boxes

Any dressing table needs these useful little boxes. Use the smallest size to store cotton wool pads or cotton buds, while the larger sizes are good for cosmetics or jewellery.

Small box

Using cols A and B held together throughout and 4 mm hook, make a yarn loop (see pages 36–37).

Rnd 1: Work 8dc into loop made and pull the loose end of yarn tight to make closed ring.

Rnd 2: Ch 1, 1dc in same st, *2dc in next st, rep from * to end, join with sl st to 1-ch (16 sts).

Rnd 3: Ch 1, 2dc in next st, *1dc in next st, 2dc in next st, rep from * to end, join with sl st to 1-ch (24 sts).

Rnd 4: Ch 1, 2dc in next st, *1dc in next st, 2dc in next st, rep from * to end, join with sl st to 1-ch (36 sts).

Rnd 5: Ch 1, 35dc, join with sl st to 1-ch .

(Rnds 6 and 7 are turning rnds, which will create an edge, changing working from base to wall of box.)

Rnd 6: Ch 1, work one rnd of sl st all around, join with sl st to 1-ch.

Rnd 7: Ch 1, work one rnd of sl st, into the outside half only of each st, join with sl st to 1-ch.

Rnd 8: Ch 1, 35dc, join with sl st to 1-ch .

Rnds 9–14: Work each as rnd 8, fasten off.

Small lid

Using cols A and B held together throughout and 4 mm hook, work as for small box until rnd 4.

Rnd 5: Ch 1, 1dc, 2dc into next st, *2dc, 2dc into next st, rep from * to end, join with sl st to 1-ch (48 sts).

Rnd 6: Ch 1, 47dc, join with sl st to 1-ch.

Rnds 7 & 8: As rnds 6 and 7 of small box.

Rnds 9 & 10: (Wall of lid) work as rnd 6, fasten off.

For the handle, attach two strands of col B into middle of box lid, ch 10, join with sl st to first ch, fasten off.

Edging

Using two lengths of col B held together throughout, join to edge of box lid.

Rnd 1: Work a rnd of dc evenly around edge of box lid.

Rnd 2: Ch 4 (counts as 1dc and 3 ch), sk 1 st, *1dc into next st, ch 3, sk 1 st, rep from * to end, join with sl st to 1-ch, fasten off.

YOU WILL NEED:

- Louisa Harding Kimono ribbon 100% nylon (93 m per 50 g ball), 3 x 50 g balls in 6 (col A) and 1 x 50 g ball in 4 (col C)
- GGH lamé 62% Viscose, 38% Polyester (192 m per 25 g ball), 1 x 25 g ball in 102 (col B)
- 4 mm hook

Note

Yarn amounts are based on average requirements and are approximate.

Large box

Using cols A and B held together throughout and 4 mm hook, work as for small box until rnd 4.

Rnd 5: Ch 1, 1dc, 2dc into next st, *2dc, 2dc into next st, rep from * to end, join with sl st to 1-ch (48 sts).

Rnd 6: Ch 1, 47dc, join with sl st to 1-ch.

Rnd 7: Ch 1, 2dc, 2dc in next st, *3dc, 2dc in next st, rep from * to end, join with sl st to 1-ch (60 sts).

Rnd 8: Ch 1, 59dc, join with sl st to 1-ch.

Rnd 9: Ch 1, 3dc, 2dc in next st, *4dc, 2dc in next st, rep from * to end, join with sl st to 1-ch (72 sts).

Rnd 10: Ch 1, 71dc, join with sl st to 1-ch.

Rnd 11: Ch 1, 4dc, 2dc in next st, *5dc, 2dc in next st, rep from * to end, join with sl st to 1-ch (84 sts).

Rnd 12: Ch 1, 83dc, join with sl st to 1-ch.

Rnd 13: Ch 1, 5dc, 2dc in next st, *6dc, 2dc in next st, rep from * to end, join with sl st to 1-ch (96 sts).

Rnd 14: Ch 1, 95dc, join with sl st to 1-ch.

Rnds 15 & 16: (Turning rnds) Work as rnds 6 & 7 of small box.

Rnds 17–23: Work each as row 14, fasten off.

Large box lid

Using cols A and B held together throughout and 4 mm hook, work as for large box until rnd 14.

Rnd 15: Ch 1, 6dc, 2dc in next st, *7dc, 2dc in next st, rep from * to end, join with sl st to 1-ch (108 sts).

Rnds 16 & 17: (Turning rnds) Work as rnds 6 & 7 of small box.

Rnd 18: Ch 1, 107dc, join with sl st to 1-ch.

Rnd 19: Rep last rnd, fasten off.

Make a tassel (see page 74) from lamé and ribbon and attach to centre of lid.

Vase-shaped trinket box

Using col C and 4 mm hook, work as for large box until rnd 7 (60 sts).

Rnds 8 & 9: (Turning rnds) Work as rnds 6 & 7 of small box.

Rnd 10: Ch 1, 59dc, join with sl st to 1-ch.

Rnds 11 & 12: As rnd 10.

Rnd 13: Ch 1, 3dc, 2dc in next st, *4dc, 2dc in next st, rep from * to end, join with sl st to 1-ch (72 sts).

Rnd 14: Ch 1, 71dc, join with sl st to 1-ch.

Rnd 15: As rnd 14, fasten off.

Rnd 16: Join in col A and B held together and dec 12 sts as follows; ch 1, 3dc, sk 1 st, (5dc, sk 1 st) 11 times, 1dc (60 sts).

Rnd 17: Ch 1, 59dc, join with sl st to 1-ch.

Rnds 18 & 19: As rnd 17, fasten off.

Rnd 20: Join in col C and dec 10 sts as follows; ch 1, 3dc, sk 1 st, (5dc, sk 1 st) 9 times, 1dc (50 sts).

Rnd 21: Ch 1, 49dc, join with sl st to 1-ch.

Rnds 22–25: As rnd 21.

Rnd 26: Dec 10 sts as follows; ch 1, 2dc, sk 1 st, (4dc, sk 1 st) 9 times, 1dc (40 sts).

Rnd 27: Ch 1, 39dc, join with sl st to 1-ch

Rnd 28: As rnd 27.

Rnd 29: Dec 8 sts as follows; ch 1, 2dc, sk 1 st, (4dc, sk 1 st) 7 times, 1dc (32 sts).

Rnd 30: Ch 1, 32dc, join with sl st to 1-ch.

Rnds 31–40: As rnd 30, fasten off.

Edging

Using two lengths of col B held together throughout, join to edge.

Rnd 1: Work a round of dc evenly around edge.

Rnd 2: Ch 3 (counts as first tr), 2tr into bottom of 3-ch, ch 3, sl st to first of this 3ch to make picot, 3tr into next st, sk 1 st, 1dc into next st, *sk 1 st, (3tr, ch 3, sl st to bottom of 3-ch to make picot, 3tr) all into next st, sk 1 st, 1dc into next st, rep from * to end of rnd, fasten off.

Table centrepiece

Decorate your table top with this mat of many circles. The pastel colours work well with the texture of wood or linen, and will protect your table from the damage that can be caused by hot dishes.

YOU WILL NEED:

- Frog Tree Alpaca 3-ply (197 m per 50 g ball), 1 x 50 g ball each of cream 000 (col A), lime green 90 (col B), and pale blue 98 (col C)
- 2.5 mm, 6 mm, and 10 mm hooks
- Tapestry needle

Note

Yarn amounts are based on average requirements and are approximate.

The mat comprises circular, wheel and floral motifs. Make different motifs as many as you like if you want a larger or smaller mat.

Flower

Make 3 or as many as for desired size of final mat.

Using 2.5 mm crochet hook and col A, ch 6, join with sl st to first ch to make ring.

Rnd 1: Ch 3 for first tr, 18tr into ring, join with sl st to top of first 3-ch.

Rnd 2: Ch 1, *1dc in next tr, ch 5, sk 1 tr, rep from * 8 times, join with sl st to first ch, fasten off.

Rnd 3: Join in col B, ch 1 (1dc, 5tr, 1dc) into 5-ch space, rep 8 times more, join with sl st to first ch, fasten off.

Wheel.

Make 8 or as many for desired size of mat.

Using 2.5 mm crochet hook and col C, make a yarn lp (see pages 36–37).

Rnd 1: Work 12dc into lp made and pull tight to make closed ring.

Rnd 2: Ch 7 (counts as first dtr and ch sp), *sk 1 dc, 1dtr into next sc, ch 3, rep from * 4 times more. Join with sl st to 3rd of first 7-ch.

Rnd 3: Ch 2 (counts as first htr), 7htr into next 3-ch sp. *8htr into next 3-ch sp, rep from * 4 more times. Join with sl st to first ch, fasten off.

Large circle

Make 20 or as many for desired size.

Using col B, wrap yarn around two fingers (or knitting needle of around size 19 mm) 28 times.

Using 2.5 mm crochet hook, work dc into ring made until all wrapped yarn is covered with dc. Join with sl st to first dc, fasten off.

Medium circle

Make as many for desired size in each col.

Wrap yarn around a size 10 mm crochet hook (or large pen) 28 times.

Using 2.5 mm crochet hook, work dc into ring until all wrapped yarn is covered with dc. Join with sl st to first dc, fasten off.

Small circle

Make as many for desired size in cols A and C.

Wrap yarn around end of 6 mm crochet hook 28 times. Using 2.5 mm crochet hook, work dc into ring until all wrapped yarn is covered with dc. Join with sl st to first dc, fasten off.

Making up

Arrange the motifs on a flat surface. Once you have a pleasing arrangement – follow the photograph for guidance if in doubt – sew each motif to the one next to it using a matching colour.

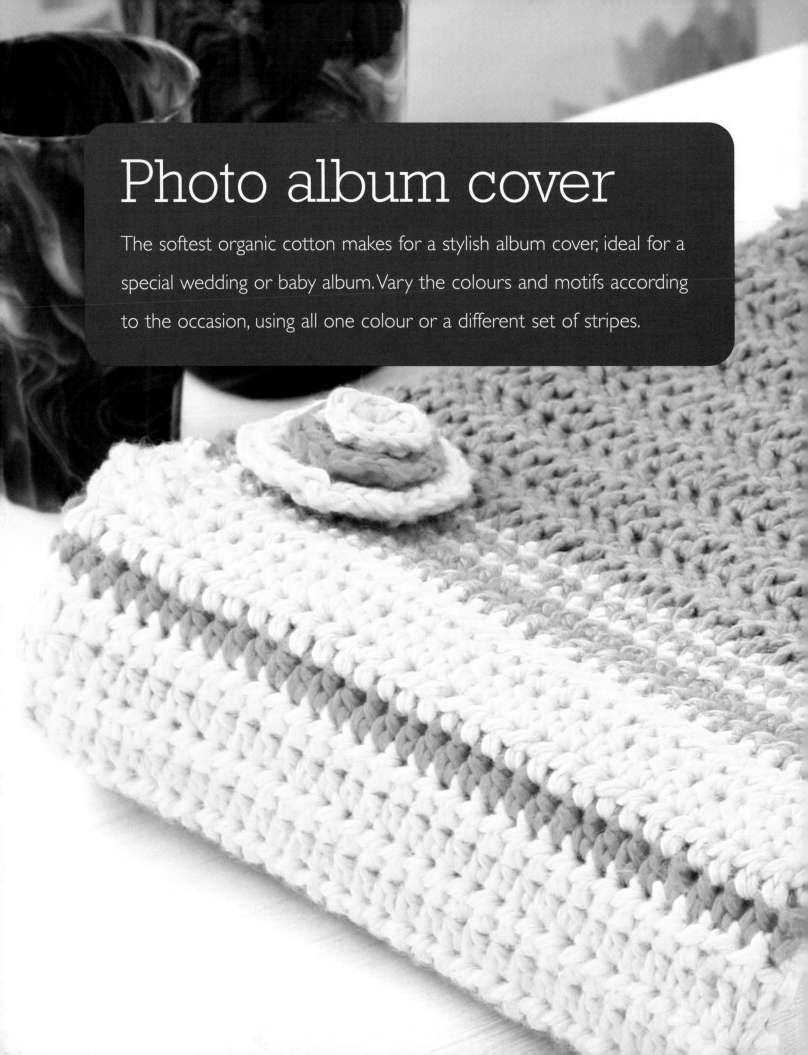

Photo album cover

The softest organic cotton makes for a stylish album cover, ideal for a special wedding or baby album. Vary the colours and motifs according to the occasion, using all one colour or a different set of stripes.

YOU WILL NEED:

- Blue sky Organic Cotton 100% cotton DK (135 m per 100 g ball), 2 x 100 g balls in lotus (col A), 2 x 100 g balls in orchid (col B), 1 x 100 g ball in lemonade (col C), 1 x 100 g ball in honeydew (col D)
- 2.5 mm and 4 mm hooks

Note
Yarn amounts are based on average requirements and are approximate.

Album cover

Using col A and 4 mm hook, ch 36, turn.
Row 1: 1tr into 4th ch from hook, tr to end (34 sts), turn.
Row 2: Ch 3 (counts as first tr), 33tr, turn.
Row 3: as row 2.
Row 4: Ch 4 (counts as first tr and 1 ch sp), sk 1 tr, 1tr into next tr, *ch1, sk 1 tr, 1tr into next tr, rep from * to end, fasten off, turn.
Row 5: Join in col B, work as row 2.
Rep last row 15 times more (20 rows), fasten off.
Row 21: Join in col C, ch 1 (counts as first dc), 33dc, fasten off, turn.
Row 22: Join in col B, work as row 21.
Row 23: Join in col D, work as row 21.
Row 24: Join in col B, work as row 21.
Row 25: Join in col A, work as row 21.
Row 26: Join in col B, work as row 21.
Row 27: Join in col C, ch 2 (counts as first htr) 33htr, fasten off, turn.
Row 28: Join in col D, work as row 27.
Row 29 & 30: Rep last 2 rows.
Row 31: Join in col A, work as row 27.
Row 32–35: As rows 27-30.
Row 36: As row 27.
Row 37: As row 31.
Row 38–41: As rows 27–30.
Row 42: Join in col B, work as row 21.
Row 43: Join in col A, work as row 21.
Row 44: Join in col B, work as row 21.
Row 45: Join in col D, work as row 21.
Row 46: Join in col B, work as row 21.
Row 47: Join in col C, work as row 21.
Row 48: Join in col B, work as row 2.
Rep last row 15 times (63 rows), fasten off.
Row 64: Join in col A, ch 4 (counts as first tr and 1 ch sp), sk 1tr, 1tr into next tr, *ch 1, sk 1tr, 1tr into next tr, rep from * to end, turn.
Rows 65–67: Work each as row 2. Fasten off.

Motif 1

Using col C and 4 mm hook, ch 4, join with a sl st to make ring.
Rnd 1: Ch 1, 7dc into ring, join with sl st to 1-ch, fasten off.
Rnd 2: Join in col C, ch 1, 1dc into same st, *2dc into next st, rep from * to end of rnd (16 sts), fasten off.
Work surface crochet (see page 71) between rnds 1 and 2 using col A.
Make 1 more using col D for first rnd and col C for 2nd rnd.

Motif 2 (make 1)

Using col C and 4 mm hook, ch 4, join with a sl st to make ring.

Rnd 1: Ch 1, 7dc into ring, join with sl st to 1-ch.

Rnd 2: Ch 1, 1dc into same st, *2dc into next st, rep from * to end of rnd (16 sts), fasten off.

Rnd 3: Ch 1, 1dc into same st, *2dc into next st, rep from * to end of rnd (32 sts), fasten off.

Motif 3

Using col A and 4 mm hook, ch 4, join with a sl st to make ring.

Rnd 1: Ch 1, 7dc into ring, join with sl st to 1-ch.

Rnd 2: Ch 1, 1dc into same st, *2dc into next st, rep from * to end of rnd (16 sts), fasten off.

Make 1 more using col C.

Motif 4

Using col D and 4 mm hook, ch 4, join with a sl st to make ring.

Rnd 1: Ch 3, 5tr into ring, join with sl st to 1-ch.

Make 4 more in col D, 3 in col C and 3 in col A.

Making up

Fold the flaps around the album to fit and sew along edges. Crochet a chain in the folds of the book to hold the album in place. Stitch together motif 2 with the motif 3 in col A and one motif 4 in col D. Stitch together the remaining motif 3 with one motif 4 in col D. Stitch the motifs onto the album cover, using the picture as a guide.

YOU WILL NEED:

- Oddments of yarn (DK and Aran) at least 3 m long for each flower
- 1 ball of green double knit yarn for the trim
- 3.75 mm hook for the trim and half the flowers, a 2 mm hook for the rest of the flowers
- Cushion pad 45 cm x 30 cm
- 1 m pink or purple silk
- Oddment of striped silk approximately 15 cm long and 1 m wide

Finished measurements
45 cm x 30 cm.

flower cushion

Shiny fabrics contrast with the yarn. Make 15 to 20 flowers of different sizes in contrasting colours for zingy effect.

Flower 1

6 ch, sl st to make ring. Make dc into ring until covered. Ch 5 then join with sl st to first st (petal made). Make loops all around the ring of 5 to 7 chain stitches depending on the weight of yarn and hook used – a smaller hook will need more stitches to make long enough petals.

Flower 2

6ch, sl st to make ring. Work dc into the ring until covered.
1 tr, sl st to first st (petal made). Ch 3 to begin the next petal, working around the ring.

Scalloped edging

Measure the outside of your cushion pad and make a chain of the same length.
Row 1: Miss 1ch, 1dc in each ch to end, 1 ch, turn.
Row 2: (1dc, 3ch, 1tr) in first dc, * miss 2dc, (1dc, 3ch, 1tr) in next dc; rep from * to last 3dc, miss 2dc, 1dc in last dc. Fasten off. Finish with a complete scallop – any stitches left can be hidden inside the cushion.

Finishing the flowers

Cut 2 circles of striped silk with a diameter 3 cm wider than each flower (the flowers will probably vary slightly in size). Fray the outside 1.5 cm of each circle, then lay the matching pairs of circles on top of each other, rotating the top one so that the stripes run in different directions on both the circles. Do not worry if the frayed edges are not exactly circular – you can trim them later. Using the end of the yarn, attach the flower to both frayed pieces. Trim the frayed edges to make a neat circle.

Making up

Cut two squares of silk the size of your cushion, with an added 1.5-cm seam allowance all around. Add a strip of matching fabric to the front, using ribbon or ric-rac to embellish the seam and top stitch. Sew the square and rectangles together along the seam allowance, RS together, trapping the crochet edging inside. The scalloped edge should point down inside the cover, so that when it is turned through the scallops will show. Leave a small opening for cushion pad, and slip stitch closed. Sew the flowers in place using either invisible stitches or a thread to match the flowers.

part 5

FASHION CROCHET

YOU WILL NEED:

- Jaeger Aqua Cotton 100% mercerized cotton (106 m per 50 g ball), 6[8:10] x 50 g balls Chrome shade 306 (col A), 1[1:2] x 50 g balls of Dust shade 324 (col B), 1[1:2] x 50 g balls of Tide shade 313 (col C)
- 4 mm crochet hook

Note
Yarn amounts are based on average requirements and are approximate.

Tension
17tr and 10 rows = 10 cm square.

Sizes
8–12[12–16:16–20]
Back length: 50[54: 58] cm.

easy all-in-one shrug

Made in one piece with no shaping, this is the ideal project even if you haven't tackled a garment before, and the pretty ruffled edging is easier to achieve than it looks. It is important to obtain the correct gauge before starting or the shrug will not be the correct size. Work a sample first, and if the tension is not correct, work another square using a smaller or larger hook. The instructions in brackets refer to the different sizes.

Shrug (worked in one piece)
Using col A and 4 mm hook ch 112[126:140], turn.
Row 1: 1tr in 4th ch from hook, tr to end (110[124:138] sts), turn.
Row 2: Ch 2 (counts as 1 tr), tr to end, turn.
Rep row 2 for 8 more rows. Place a marker at each end of last row.
Cont for a further 34[38:42] rows. Place a marker at each end of last row.
Cont for a further 8 rows (work measures, 50[54:58] cm), fasten off.

Making up
Work in all loose ends. Block and press the work. Fold shrug in half lengthways, and pin RS together. Using a tapestry needle threaded with matching yarn, join the yarn at one end of the side seam and over sew the seam edges up to the markers; fasten off. Join the yarn to the side seam at the other end of the shrug and stitch the seam up to the other markers; fasten off.

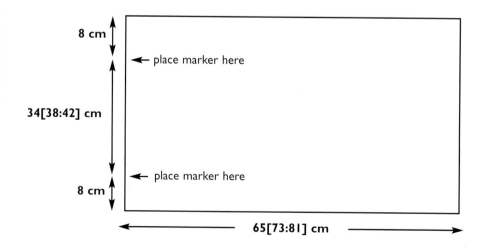

8 cm

← place marker here

34[38:42] cm

← place marker here

8 cm

65[73:81] cm

Armhole edging

Using col A and 4 mm hook, rejoin yarn to work to armhole at marked end of one seam, with RS facing.

Rnd 1: Ch 1 (counts as 1st dc), work 61[71:81] dc evenly around armhole opening, join with sl st to top of 1-ch, joining col B by pulling through last lp of sl st, break off col A.

Rnd 2: Working in front lp only of every st, *sl st into next dc, ch 6, sl st back into same st, rep from * to end, join with sl st to top of 1-ch, joining col C by pulling through last lp of sl st, break off col B.

Rnd 3: Working in back lp only of every st, *sl st into next dc, ch 8, sl st back into same st, rep from * to end, fasten off.

Work 2nd armhole to match first.

Neckline

Using col A and 4 mm hook rejoin yarn to neckline at a seam, with RS facing.

Rnd 1: Ch 1 (counts as 1st dc), work 220[248:276] dc evenly around neckline, join with sl st to top of 1-ch, joining col B by pulling through last lp of sl st, break off col A.

Rnd 2: Working in front lp only of every st, work as follows: *sl st into next dc, ch 6, sl st back into same st, rep from * to end, join with sl st to top of 1-ch, joining col C by pulling through last lp of sl st, break off col B.

Rnd 3: Working in back lp only of every st, *sl st into next dc, ch 8, sl st back into same st, rep from * to end, fasten off. Work in all loose ends.

Ruffle edging

This simple edging is worked in groups of 6 chain stitches. One colour is worked into the front loops of the edge stitches, and the second contrast colour is worked into the back loops (see page 65).

crossover cardigan

This flattering wrap-cardigan combines a simple filet stitch with surface embroidery. Buttons are added in a contrasting colour to match the two-tone edgings.

Sizes

To fit sizes: 8–10[12–14:16–18:20–22]
Actual bust: 86[96:107:119] cm
Back length: 59[61:63:65] cm
Underarm seam: 34[35:36:37] cm

Figures in square brackets refer to larger sizes; where there is only one set of figures this applies to all sizes.

Back

Using col A and 4 mm hook, ch 84[94:104:114].

Row 1: 1tr into 6th ch from hook (first 5 ch counts as 1tr, ch 1, sk 1), ch 1, *1tr, ch 1, sk 1 ch, rep from * to last ch, 1tr (81[91:101:111] sts and 40[45:50:55] ch sps), turn.

Row 2: Ch 3 (counts as 1 tr, 1 ch), sk 1 tr, ch 1, *1tr in next tr, ch 1, sk 1 ch sp, rep from *, ending with 1tr in 4th of 5-ch at beg of prev row, turn.

Row 3: Ch 3 (counts as 1tr, 1ch), sk 1 tr, ch 1, * 1 tr in next tr, ch 1, sk 1 ch sp, rep from *, ending 1tr in top of 2-ch at beg of prev row, turn.

Rep row 3 to form treble grid pattern.

Cont in patt until work measures 14[15:16:17] cm.

Next row: Ch 2 (counts as dec over 2 sts, do not work into this st at the end of the next row), sk 1 tr, ch 1, work in patt to last 3 sts, dec over 3 sts (38[43:48:53] ch sp), turn.

Cont in patt until work measures 32[33:34:35] cm.

Shape Armholes

Next row: Sl st over 4[4:6:6] sts, ch 2 (counts as dec over 2 sts, do not work into this st at the end of the next row), sk 1 tr, ch 1, work in patt to within 9[11:11:12] sts of end of row, dec over 3 sts, turn.

Next row: Ch 2 (counts as dec over 2 sts, do not work into this st at the end of the next row), sk 1 tr, ch 1, work in patt to within 3 sts of end of row, dec over 3 sts (30[35:38:43] ch sp), turn.

Cont in patt until work measures 55[57:59:61] cm.

Shape Shoulders

Next row: Sl st over 6[8:8:9] sts, ch 2 (counts as dec over 2 sts, do not work into this st at the end of the next row), sk 1 tr, ch 1, work in patt to within 9[11:11:12] sts of end of row, dec over 3 sts, turn.

YOU WILL NEED:

- Rowan Scottish Tweed DK 100% wool (113 m per 50 g ball), 8[9:11:12] x 50 g balls shade 017 Lobster (col A), 1[1:2:2] x 50 g balls shade 011 Sunset (col B), 1[1:2:2:2] x 50 g balls shade 015 Apple (col C)
- 4 mm crochet hook
- Tapestry needle
- Approximately 40 x 1 cm buttons

Note

Yarn amounts are based on average requirements and are approximate.

Tension

18 sts and 9 rows = 10 cm measured over filet grid using 4 mm hook.

Special abbreviations

dec over 3 sts – work thus: *yrh insert into next st, draw through a loop, yrh draw through 2 loops, sk next ch, then rep from *, yrh, draw through 3 loops on hook.

Next row: Sl st over 8[10:10:13] sts, ch 2 (counts as dec over 2 sts, do not work into this st at the end of the next row), sk 1 tr, ch 1, work in patt to within 11[13:13:16] sts of end of row, dec over 3 sts (25[27:33:35] sts rem for back neck), fasten off.

Front (work 2 the same)

Using col A and 4 mm hook, ch 64[68:70:74]. Work as given for rows 1–3 of the back (61[65:67:71] sts).

Cont in patt as given for the 3rd row until work measures 14[15:16:17] cm.

Next row: (Beg at armhole edge) ch 2 (counts as dec over 2 sts, do not work into this st at the end of the next row), sk 1 tr, ch 1, work in patt to end.

Next row: (Beg at centre edge) ch 2 (counts as dec over 2 sts, do not work into this st at the end of the next row), sk 1 tr, ch 1, work in patt to end.

Next row: Work in patt.

Rep the last 2 rows 16 times and, AT SAME TIME, work armhole shapings as follows, when work measures 32[33:34:35] cm, ending at armhole edge.

Armhole Shapings

Next row: Sl st over 4[4:6:6] sts, ch 2 ch (counts as dec over 2 sts, do not work into this st at the end of the next row), sk 1 tr, ch 1, work in patt to end, turn.

Next row: Patt to within 3 sts of end of row, dec over next 3 stitches, turn.

Cont as before, keeping armhole edge straight and continuing to shape at centre edge until the 16 dec have been made.

Cont without shaping at neck edge until work measures 55[57:59:61] cm, ending at neck edge, turn.

Shape Shoulders

Next row: Patt to within 9[11:11:12] sts of end of row, dec over 3 sts, turn.

Next row: Ch 2 (counts as dec over 2 sts) sk 1 tr, ch 1, patt to end, fasten off.

Sleeves (make 2 the same)

Using col A and 4 mm hook ch 48[50:52:54].

Work as given for rows 1–3 of the back (45[47:49:51] sts).

Cont in patt and, AT SAME TIME, inc 1 st at each end of the 3rd and every foll 3rd row until there are 69[73:77:81] sts.

Then cont without shaping until work measures 42[43:44:45] cm, turn.

Shape Top

Next row: Sl st over 4[4:6:6] sts, ch 2 (counts as dec over 2 sts, do not work into this st at the end of the next row), sk 1 tr, ch 1, work in patt to within 7[7:9:9] sts of end of row, dec over 3 sts, turn.

Next row: Ch 2 (counts as dec over 2 sts, do not work into this st at the end of the next row), sk 1 tr, ch 1, work in patt to within 3 sts of end of row, dec over 3 sts, turn.

Next row: Ch 2 (counts as dec over 2 sts, do not work into this st at the end of the next row), sk 1 tr, ch 1, work in patt to within 3 sts of end of row, dec over 3 sts, turn.

Next row: Patt to end (49[53:53:57] ch sp), turn.

Rep the last 2 rows 6 more times.

Next row: Sl st over 4 sts, ch 2 (counts as dec over 2 sts), sk 1 tr, ch 1, work in patt to within 7 sts of end of row, dec over 3 sts, turn.

Rep last row 0[1:1:1] more time, fasten off.

Short belt

Using col A and 4 mm hook ch 55[65:75:85].

Row 1: 1dc in 3rd ch from hook, dc to end, joining in col B by pulling through last lp, break col A yarn, turn.

Row 2: Work in col B as for first row but change to col C at end of row, turn.

Row 3: Work in col C as for first row, but change to col A at end of row, turn.

Row 4: Work in col A as for first row, fasten off.

Long belt

Using col A and 4 mm hook ch 114[124:134:144].

Work as given for the short belt.

Cuffs (work both the same)

Using col B and 4 mm hook, join yarn to lower edge of sleeve, at the seam and on RS of work.

Rnd 1: Ch 1 (counts as 1dc), work 1dc into each st around lower edge of sleeve, break yarn and, using col C, sl st to top of 1-ch, turn.

Rnd 2: Work in col C as for first rnd, but change to col A at end of rnd, turn.

Rnd 3: Work in col A as for first rnd, fasten off.

Frontband

Using col B and 4 mm hook, join yarn to bottom edge of cardigan at the right side seam and on RS of work.

Row 1: Ch 1 (counts as 1dc), work 60[63:66:70] dc to first corner, work 3dc into corner, work 27[31:35:39] dc along straight edge of right front, then place marker in the next st worked. Cont and work 75[79:83:87] dc to within 1 cm of shoulder seam. Then (work 2dc dec, 1dc) 3 times. Work 12[14:18:20] dc, then work (1dc, work 2dc dec) 3 times. Cont and work 75[79:83:87] dc to beg of straight edge on left front, then place marker in the last st worked. Cont and work 27[31:35:39] dc along straight edge, work 3dc into corner, work 59[63:66:70] dc to left side seam. Cont and work 79[90:100:110] dc round the back of the cardigan to beg of edging at right seam. Break yarn and, using col C, sl st to top of 1-ch, turn.

Row 2: Work as row 1, using col C, working 3dc into each corner and 2dc into each of the marked sts. Change to col A at end of row.

Row 3: Work in col A as for row 2, fasten off. Work in all loose ends.

Making up

Block each piece and steam very lightly (do not press). Work in all the ends. Pin the right front and back RS together. Using a tapestry needle threaded with matching yarn, over sew the side seam, leaving a 3 cm gap 14[15:16:17] cm up from lower edge. Ensure that the seam lies flat. Repeat to stitch the left front and back together. Stitch the shoulder seams. Fold the sleeves in half lengthways, RS together, and stitch along the seam. Set the sleeves into the cardigan, RS together, and stitch in place. Stitch the short belt to top of straight edge on right front, lining it up with the gap in the seam. Sew the long belt to top of straight edge on left front so it is lined up with the short belt.

Using photo on page 110 as a guide, work lazy-daisy embroidery stitches around the grid pattern at intervals, alternating between colours C and B. Sew a button onto the centre of each lazy-daisy flower.

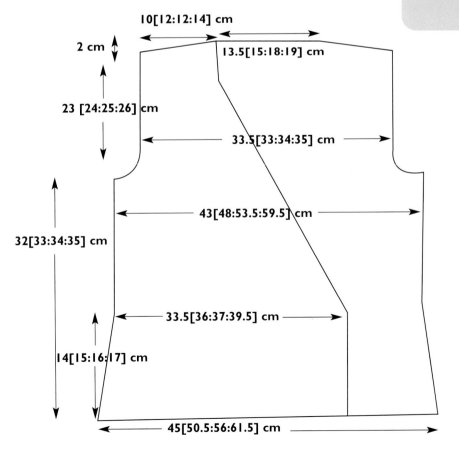

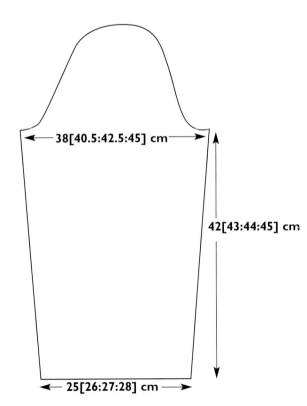

YOU WILL NEED:

- Patons 100% Cotton DK 100 % wool (210 m per 100 g ball), 3[4:5] x 100 g balls Denim shade 02697
- 5 mm and 4 mm hooks
- Selection of beads
- Tapestry needle
- Approximately 40 x 1 cm buttons

Note

Yarn amounts are based on average requirements and are approximate.

Tension

20 sts and 22 rows over dc = 10 cm square.
2 patt reps and 11 rows = 10 cm square.

Special abbreviations

Cr (work corner): work a corner thus: yrh, insert hook into next st. Yrh, draw through a lp, yrh. Insert hook in corner, yrh, draw through a lp. Yrh, insert hook into next st, yrh draw through a lp. Yrh, draw through all 4 lps on hook.

lacy blue camisole

Lacy stitches will keep you cool on the hottest sunny day. This pretty top looks great with jeans or dressed up with a jacket for a warm summer's evening out.

Sizes

To fit bust: 80–85[85–90:90–95] cm
Finished measurement under bust 90[95:100] cm
Back length: 30[33:35] cm
Figures in square brackets refer to larger sizes; where there is only one set of figures this applies to all sizes.

Camisole

Using 4 mm hook ch 180[190:200], join with a sl st to first ch to make a ring.
Rnd 1: Ch 3 (counts as 1tr, ch 1), *1tr in next ch, ch 1, sk 1 ch, rep from * to end, sl st to 2nd of 3-ch at beg of rnd, taking care not to twist work (90[95:100] ch sp), turn.
Rnd 2: Ch 2 (counts as 1tr), 1tr, *ch 4, sk 3 sts, 1dc, ch 4, sk 3 sts, 3tr, rep from * to last rep, ending last rep with 1tr in last st of rnd, sl st to top of 2-ch at beg of rnd, (18[19:20] patt reps), turn.
Rnd 3: Ch 2 (counts as 1tr), 1tr, *ch 1, 1dc in next ch sp, ch 4, 1dc in next ch sp, ch 1, 3tr, rep from * to last rep, ending last rep with 1tr in last st of rnd, sl st to top of 2-ch at beg of rnd, turn.
Rnd 4: Ch 2 (counts as 1tr), 1tr, *7tr in 3-ch sp, 3tr, rep from * to last rep, ending last rep with 1tr in last st of rnd, sl st to top of 2-ch at beg of rnd, turn.
Rnd 5: Ch 2 (counts as 1tr), 1tr *ch 3, 1dc in 4th of 7-tr group, ch 3, 3tr, rep from * to last rep, ending last rep with 1tr in last st of rnd, sl st to top of 2-ch at beg of rnd, turn.
Rnds 3–5 form the pattern. Cont in patt until work measures 30[33:36] cm, ending with a 4th patt rnd; fasten off.

Bra cups (make 2 the same)

Using 4 mm hook, ch 13[17:21], turn.
Row 1: 1dc in 3rd ch from hook, dc to end (12[16:20] sts), turn.
Row 2: Ch 1 (counts as 1dc), 11[15:19] dc, 1dc into side of first ch of prev row (mark this centre stitch with a coloured thread and move it up with every row). Do not turn; work 12[16:20] dc along base of the foundation ch, join with sl st to 1-ch at beg of row; do not turn.
Row 3: Ch 1 (counts as 1dc), 11[15:19] dc, 5dc into marked centre st (mark the 3rd of these dc), 12[16:20] dc, join with sl st to 1-ch at beg of row; do not turn.
Row 4: Ch 1 (counts as 1dc), 13[17:21] dc, 5dc into marked centre st (mark the 3rd of these dc), 14[18:22] dc, join with sl st to 1-ch at beg of row; do not turn.

Row 5: Ch 1 (counts as 1dc), 15[19:23] dc, 3dc into marked centre st (mark the 2nd of these dc), 16[20:24] dc, join with sl st to 1-ch at beg of row; do not turn.

Row 6: Ch 1 (counts as 1dc), 16[20:24] dc, 3dc into marked centre st (mark the 2nd of these dc), 17[21:25] dc, join with sl st to 1-ch at beg of row; do not turn.

Row 7: Ch 1 (counts as 1dc), 17[21:25] dc, 1dc into marked centre st (mark this st), 18[22:26] dc, join with sl st to 1-ch at beg of row; do not turn.

Row 8: Ch 1 (counts as 1dc), 17[21:25] dc, 3dc into marked centre st (mark the 2nd of these dc), 18[22:26] dc, join with sl st to 1-ch at beg of row; do not turn (39[47:55] sts).

Row 9: Ch 2 (counts as 1tr), 6[8:10] tr, 6[7:8] htr, 6[7:8] dc, 1dc into marked centre st (mark this st), 6[7:8] dc, 6[7:8] htr, 7[9:11] tr, join with sl st to top of 2-ch at beg of row; do not turn.

Row 10: Ch 2 (counts as tr), 6[8:10] tr, 6[7:8] htr, 6[7:8] dc, 3dc into marked centre st (mark the 2nd of these dc), 6[7:8] dc, 6[7:8] htr, 7[9:11] tr, join with sl st to top of 2-ch at beg of row; do not turn.

Row 11: Ch 2 (counts as 1tr), 6[8:10] tr, 6[7:8] htr, 7[8:9] dc, 1dc into marked centre st (mark this st), 7[8:9] dc, 6[7:8] htr, 7[9:11] tr, join with sl st to top of 2-ch at beg of row; do not turn.

Row 12: Ch 2 (counts as 1tr), 6[8:10] tr, 6[7:8] htr, 7[8:9] dc, 3dc into marked centre st (mark the 2nd of these dc), 7[8:9] dc, 6[7:8] htr, 7[9:11] tr, join with sl st to top of 2-ch at beg of row; do not turn (43[51:59] sts).

2nd and 3rd sizes only:

Row 13: Ch 2 (counts as 1tr), 8[10] tr, 7[8] htr, 9[10] dc, 1dc into marked centre st (mark this st), 9[10] dc, 7[8] htr, 9[11] tr, join with sl st to top of 2-ch at beg of row; do not turn (51[59] sts).

Row 14: Ch 2 (counts as 1tr), 8[10] tr, 7[8] htr, 9[10] dc, 3dc into marked centre st (mark the 2nd of these dc), 9[10] dc, 7[8] htr, 9[11] tr, join with sl st to top of 2-ch at beg of row; do not turn (53[61] sts).

3rd size only:

Row 15: Ch 2 (counts as 1tr), 10tr, 8htr, 11dc, 1dc into marked centre st (mark this st), 11dc, 9htr, 11tr, join with sl st to top of 2-ch at beg of row; do not turn (61 sts).

Row 16: Ch 2 (counts as 1tr), 10tr, 8htr, 11dc, 3dc into marked centre st (mark the 2nd of these dc), 11dc, 9htr, 11tr, join with sl st to top of 2-ch at beg of row; do not turn (63 sts).

All sizes:

Next row: Ch 2 (counts as 1 tr), 20[25:30] tr, 3tr in centre st (mark the 2nd of these dc), 21[26:31] tr, join with sl st to top of 2-ch at beg of row, fasten off.

Making up

Block and lightly press the pieces of work. Lay the camisole out flat so that the beg of rnds falls at one side. Find the patt rep that falls at the centre front – mark the centre of this patt rep. Pin the bra cups to the top edge of the camisole, RS together, positioning the cups on either side of the marked point and leaving a 1 cm gap between them. Using a tapestry needle threaded with matching yarn, over sew the seams so that they lie flat. Mark the centre point of the back on the top edge.

Edging

Using 4 mm hook, rejoin yarn at marked point on back of camisole, RS facing, and work around edge as follows:

Row 1: Ch 1 (counts as first dc), work 49[55:61] dc up to the 3 sts at corner of bra top, **1cr (see page 114) into these 3 sts, work 21[26:31] dc along first side of bra cup, 3dc in marked centre st, 21[26:31] sts, 1cr**, 3dc along top edge. Then work as given from ** to ** once more. Work 49[55:61] dc to marker, join with sl st to 1-ch (201[233:265] sts), turn.

Row 2: Work shell pattern thus; sl st into first dc, (sk 2dc, 5tr into next dc, sk 2dc, sl st into next dc) 8[9:10] times, **1cr into the 3 corner sts, sk 2[1:0] dc; sl st into next dc, (sk 2dc, 5tr into next dc, sk 2dc, sl st into next dc) 3[4:5] times, 7tr in marked centre st, sl st into next dc, (sk 2dc, 5tr into next dc, sk 2dc, sl st into next dc) 3[4:5] times, sk 2[1:0] dc, 1cr into the 3 corner sts**, 1dc. Rep from ** to **. (Sk 2dc, 5tr into next dc, sk 2dc, sl st into next dc)

8[9:10] times, sl st to first sl st of round, fasten off. Mark the point 3 shells to the right of the centre back point, then mark the point 3 shells to the left.

Shoulder Straps (make 2)

Using the yarn doubled and 5 mm hook, make a ch 53 [55: 57] cm long, leaving a long length of loose yarn at the beginning. Fasten off and leave a long length of loose yarn at the end.

Making up

Using the loose ends threaded on to a tapestry needle, sew one end of one strap to the centre point of the left-hand bra cup. Sew the other end of the strap to the marked point that's right of the centre back. Sew the other strap to the right-hand bra cup. Sew the end of this strap to the marked point left of the centre back. The straps will cross over at the back of the camisole.

This is a close-up of the lacy pattern. You can ring the changes by using a contrasting colour for the shoulder straps and tie cord.

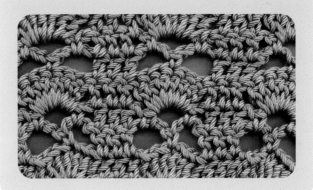

Tie cord

Using the yarn doubled and 5 mm hook, make a ch 150 [155: 160] cm long, leaving a long length of loose yarn at the beginning. Fasten off and leave a long length of loose yarn at the end.

Thread the tie through the first row of the camisole, from centre front round to centre front. Finish the ends of the tie with a selection of beads. Work in loose ends.

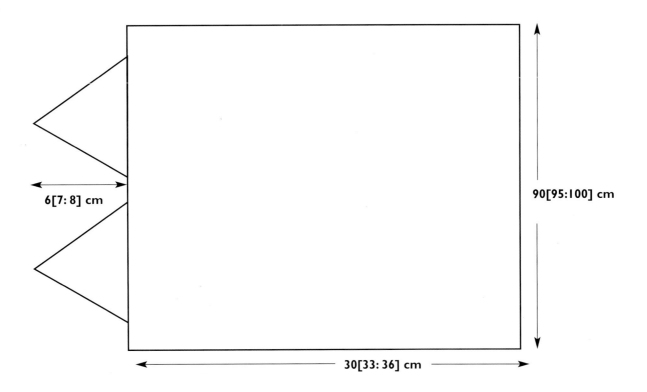

6[7: 8] cm

90[95:100] cm

30[33: 36] cm

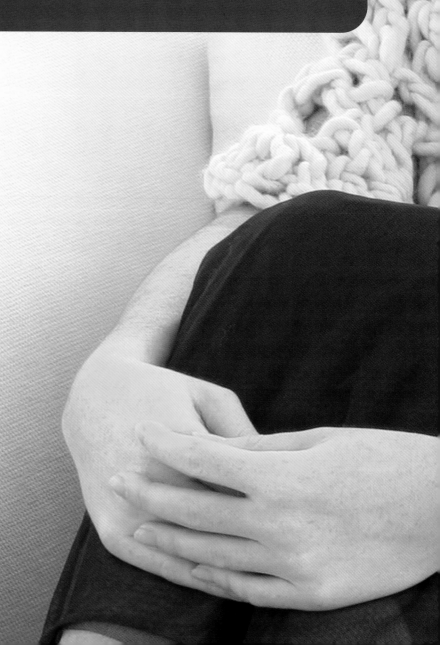

Peace-pink alpaca shawl

Made from the softest hand-dyed alpaca, this shawl will keep out the chills, and is soft enough to wear against your skin with an evening outfit. The huge size of the hook means the project will grow quickly.

YOU WILL NEED:

- Blue Sky Alpaca Chunky Hand-dye, 50% alpaca, 50% wool (41 m per 100 g hank), 6 x 100 g hanks in Peace Pink
- 19 mm hook
- Tapestry needle

Tension

1 patt rep and 3 rows = 18 x 10 cm using 19 mm crochet hook over fan patt.

Special abbreviations

Fan = 5tr in same st.

Notes

The shawl is a basic triangle, worked from widest to narrowest point. Yarn amounts given are based on average requirements and are approximate.

Shawl

Using 19 mm hook, ch 54, turn.

Row 1: 1dc in 3rd ch from hook, dc to end, turn.

Row 2: Ch 3, sk 2dc, *5tr in next dc, 1dc, ch 1, sk 1dc, 1dc, sk 2dc rep from * until 7 fans made, 1tr in last dc, turn.

Row 3: Ch 2, *1dc in centre st of fan, ch 2, sk 2tr, (1tr, ch 1, 1tr) into next 1-ch sp, sk 2 tr, ch 2, rep from * to end, 1dc in centre st of fan, ch 2, 1dc in top of 3-ch, turn.

Row 4: Ch 3, sk 2ch, *5tr in next dc, (1dc, ch 1, 1dc) into next 1-ch sp, rep from * until 7 fans made, 1tr in top of 2-ch, turn.

Row 5: Sl st to centre st of first fan, ch 1 (counts as first dc), *ch 2, sk 2tr, (1tr, ch 1, 1tr) into next 1-ch sp, sk 2 ch, 1dc, rep from * to end, with last dc in centre of last fan, turn.

Row 6: Ch 3, *sk 2ch and 1tr, (1dc, ch 1, 1dc) into next 1-ch sp, sk 1tr and 2ch, 5tr in next tr, rep from * until 5 fans made, sk 2ch and 1tr, (1dc, ch 1, 1dc) into next 1-ch sp, 1tr in last dc, turn.

Row 7: As row 4.

Row 8: As row 5.

Row 9: Sl st to 1-ch sp (the sp made by 1dc, ch 1, 1dc on last row), ch 4, 1tr in same sp, *sk 2tr, ch 2, 1dc in centre st of fan, ch 2, sk 2tr, (1tr, ch 1, 1tr) into next 1-ch sp, rep from * to end.

Row 10: Ch 3, 1dc into next 1-ch sp, sk 1tr and 2 ch, 5tr in next tr, rep from * until 5 fans made, sk 2ch and 1tr, (1dc, ch 1, 1dc) into last 1-ch sp, turn.

Row 11: As row 8.

Row 12: As row 9.

Row 13: As row 4.

Row 14: As row 5 (but only 3 fans made).

Row 15: As row 8.

Row 16: As row 9 (but only 3 fans made).

Row 17: Sl st to 1-ch sp (the sp made by 1dc, ch 1, 1dc on last row), ch 4, 1tr in same sp, * sk 2tr, ch 2, 1dc in centre st of fan, ch 2, sk 2tr, (1tr, ch 1, 1tr) into next 1-ch sp, rep from * to end.

Row 18: Ch 3, 1dc into 1-ch sp, sk 1tr and 2 ch, 5tr in next tr, sk 2ch and 1tr, (1dc, 1ch, 1dc) all in last 1ch sp, fasten off.

Edging

Rejoin yarn to right hand of top edge, with RS facing, and work 1dc in each dc along edge. Turn the corner to work along the diagonal edge of the shawl thus: *1dc in edge, sk about 3–4 cm of the edge, then 5tr into edge, rep from * until you have made 7 fans along this diagonal side. The last dc should be made in the 1-ch sp next to the last fan. Then work 5tr in centre st of fan and 1dc in 1-ch sp next to the fan. Work fans and dc and fans along the rem side to correspond with first diagonal. End with a sl st to first dc; fasten off.

Tip

When working fans along the edge of the shawl, you could mark the position of each 5tr by inserting 7 pins along the edge at evenly spaced intervals. Then work the 5tr at each pin, with 1dc worked equally between each fan.

Finishing

Work in any loose ends. Steam lightly to shape. Make 3 oversized tassels (see page 74) and using the same yarn, and an oversized needle, attach one at each corner.

chevron crochet skirt

This modern hip-hugging skirt will shimmy and sway as you walk. With not one, but two waist pockets to keep your MP3 player and your phone near you, you will have your hands free for more important things.

YOU WILL NEED:

- Jaeger Matchmaker Merino DK 100% merino wool (120 m per 50 g ball), 9[9:10:10:11] x 50 g balls in Granite shade 639 (col A), 3[3:4:4:5] x 50 g balls in Rosy shade 870 (col B)
- 4 mm hook

Tension
18 sts and 15 rows = 10 cm using 4 mm hook over htr.

Finished measurements
To fit hip (actual hip): 80 [86.5:93.5:100:106.5] cm. Back length: 33.5[37:38.5:41.5:42.5] cm. Figures in square brackets refer to larger sizes; where there is only one set of figures this applies to all sizes.

Skirt (worked in one piece)

Using col A and 4 mm hook ch 144[156:168:180:192], join with a sl st to first ch to make a ring.

Foundation rnd: (Take care not to twist work) ch 2 (counts as first st), sk first ch, htr to end, sl st to top of 2-ch at beg of row, (144[156:168:180:192] sts), turn.

Rnd 1: Ch 2 (counts as first st), sk first st, htr to end, sl st to top of 2-ch at beg of row, turn.

Rnd 2: (Make eyelets for belt) ch 2 (counts as first st), sk first st, *5[5:6:7:7] tr, ch 1, sk next st, 6[7:7:7:8] tr, rep from * to end, finishing with ending 5[6:6:6:7] tr, sl st to top of 2-ch at beg of row (12 eyelets formed), turn.

Rep rnd 1 for a further 16[16:18:18:20] rnds, turn.

Next rnd: (Foundation row for chevrons) ch 4 (counts as first st), sk first st *(1dtr, 1tr) into next st, 1tr, 2htr into next st, 2dc, sl st to next st, 2dc, 2htr into next st, 1tr, (1tr, 1dtr) into next st, 1dtr, rep from * to end, omitting last dtr of the last rep, sl st to top of 4-ch at beg of rnd (12[13:14:15:16] patt repeats), turn.

Work in chevron pattern as follows:

Rnd 1: Ch 2 (counts as first st), 2htr into base of same st, *6htr, sk next 3 sts, 6htr, 5htr into next st, rep from * to end of rnd, ending last rep with 2htr into base of first st, sl st to top of 2-ch at beg of rnd, turn.

Rnd 2: Ch 2 (counts as first st), 1 htr in base of this st, *7htr, sk next 2 sts, 7htr, 3htr in next st, rep from * to end of rnd, ending last rep with 1htr in base of first st, sl st to top of 2-ch at beg of rnd, turn.

Rnd 3: Ch 2 (counts as first st), 2htr in base of this st, *7htr, sk next 2 sts, 7htr, 5htr into next st, rep from * to end of rnd, ending last rep with 2htr into base of first st, sl st to top of 2-ch at beg of rnd, turn.

Rnd 4: Ch 2 (counts as first st), 1htr in base of this st, *8htr, sk next 2 sts, 8htr, 3htr in next st, rep from * to end, ending last rep with 1htr into base of first st, break yarn and join in col B, sl st to top of 2-ch at beg of rnd, turn.

Rnd 5: Rep last row, using col B, but joining in col A at end of rnd, turn.

Rnd 6: Ch 2 (counts as first st), 2htr into base of this st, *8htr, sk next 2 sts, 8htr, 5htr into next st, rep from * to end of rnd, ending last rep 2htr into base of first st, sl st to top of 2-ch at beg of rnd, turn.

Rnd 7: Ch 2 (counts as first st), 1htr in base of this st, *9htr, sk next 2 sts, 9htr, 3htr in next st, rep from * to end, ending last rep 2htr into base of first st, sl st to top of 2-ch at beg of rnd, turn.

Rnd 8: Ch 2 (counts as first st), 2htr into base of this st, *9htr, sk next 2 sts, 9htr, 5htr into next st, rep from * to end of rnd, ending last rep 2htr into base of first st, sl st to top of 2-ch at beg of rnd, turn.

Rnd 9: Ch 2 (counts as first st), 1htr in base of this st, *10htr, sk next 2 sts, 10htr, 3htr in next st, rep from * to end of rnd, ending last rep 1htr into base of first st, break yarn and join in col B, sl st to top of 2-ch at beg of rnd, turn.

Rnd 10: Rep last row, using col B, but joining in col A at end of rnd, turn.

Cont in the foll way:

Work 30[35:35:40:40] rnds. On rnds 11, 13, 16, 18, 21, 23, 26, 28, 31, 33, 36 and 38 work as for the 8th rnd but work one more htr along each diagonal of the chevrons than the prev rnd. On rnds 12, 14, 17, 19, 22, 24, 27, 29, 32, 34, 37, 39 work as for the 9th rnd but work the same number of htr along each diagonal of the chevrons as the prev rnd. On rnds 15, 20, 25, 30, 35 and 40 rep the prev rnd using col B. Fasten off.

Belt

Using col B and 4 mm hook, ch 221[235:253:269:285].

Row 1: 1htr into 3rd ch from hook, htr to end (220[234:252:268:284] sts), turn.

Row 2: Ch 2 (counts as first st), sk first st, htr to end. Fasten off.

Making up

Sew in all the ends and lightly steam all the pieces with a warm iron. Thread the belt through the eyelets, passing it through the looped straps of the pockets, to attach these at the desired position.

Small pocket

Using col A and 4 mm hook, ch 13, turn.

Row 1: 1htr in 3rd ch from hook, htr to end (12 sts), turn.

Row 2: Ch 2 (counts as first st), htr to end, turn.

Rep row 2 for 18 more rows. Mark each end of the last row with coloured thread, then cont for a further 19 rows.
Next row: Ch 2 (counts as first st), 2htr (3 sts), turn. Working on these 3 sts only, rep the prev row for 18 more rows. Mark each end of the last row with coloured thread, then cont for a further 8 rows. Fasten off. Rejoin yarn to opposite edge of the pocket and rep from ** to **.

To make up:

Fold up the pocket section at the first marker. Using col B and 4 mm hook, join the yarn at the fold on one edge. Work dc through both edges to join together. Cont in dc all around the edge of the strap, along the top edge of the pocket, around the second strap and then back down the other side of the pocket to join the edges together; fasten off. Fold the straps at the markers, to the inside of the pocket and stitch in place with a tapestry needle threaded with a length of matching yarn.

Large pocket

Using col A and 4 mm hook, ch 21.

Row 1: 1htr in 3rd ch from hook, htr to end (20 sts), turn.

Row 2: Ch 2 (counts as first st), htr to end, turn.

Rep row 2 for 20 more rows. Mark each end of the last row with coloured thread,
Next row: Ch 2 (counts as first st), 3htr (4 sts), turn. Working on these 4 sts only, rep the prev row for 16 more rows. Mark each end of the last row with coloured thread, then cont for a further 8 rows. Fasten off. Rejoin yarn to opposite edge of the pocket and rep from ** to **.

Make up and work edging as for the small pocket.

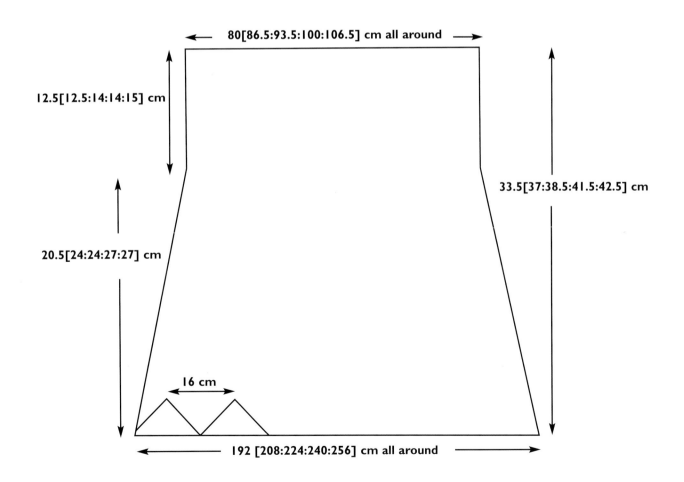

80[86.5:93.5:100:106.5] cm all around

12.5[12.5:14:14:15] cm

33.5[37:38.5:41.5:42.5] cm

20.5[24:24:27:27] cm

16 cm

192 [208:224:240:256] cm all around

Chunky hooded jacket

Even though it has a lacy design, this jacket will keep you as warm as toast. The beautiful variegated Noro yarn is a blend of luxurious yarn types and toning colours that won't fail to please.

YOU WILL NEED:

- Noro Transitions, 55% wool, 10% silk, 7% angora, 7% cashmere, 7% alpaca, 7% kid mohair, 7% camel (120 m per 100 g skein), 9 [9:10:10:11] × 100 g balls in colour 7
- Brooch or kilt pin
- 7.5 mm crochet hook
- Tapestry needle

Tension

11 sts and 13 rows = 10 cm using 7.5 mm hook over dc. 2 patt reps and 8 rows = 11 cm x 10 cm using 7.5 mm hook over patt.

Sizes

S–M [M–L: L–XL]
Bust:
80–90[90–100:100–110] cm
Actual bust:
100 [110:130] cm
Centre back:
63 [63:69] cm
Sleeve seam:
42.5 [47.5:47.5] cm

Body (worked sideways in one piece)

Using 7.5 mm hook, ch 69[69:75], turn.

Work in pattern as follows:

Row 1 (RS): 1dc into 3rd ch from hook, *ch 6, sk 4ch, 2dc, rep from * to end (11[11:12] patt reps), turn.

Row 2: Ch 2 (counts as first tr), sk first dc, 1tr in next dc, *ch 2, 1dc into 6-ch lp, ch 2, 2tr, rep from * to end, turn.

Row 3: Ch 2 (counts as first tr), sk first tr, 1tr into next tr, *ch 3, sl st into next dc, ch 3, 2tr, rep from * to end, turn.

Row 4: Ch 1 (counts as first dc), sk first tr, 1dc into next tr, *ch 4, 1dc into each of next 2 tr, rep from * to end, turn.

Row 5: Ch 1 (counts as first dc), sk first dc, 1dc into next dc, *ch 6, 1dc into each of next 2dc, rep from * to end, turn.

Rows 2 to 5 form the pattern. Cont in patt until work measures 10[15:20] cm. Place a marker on one side edge; this marks the hood at the neck edge. Cont in patt until work measures 20[25:30] cm, ending with a 4th (WS) patt row at the neck edge.

**Ch 7, turn and work 1 dc in 3rd ch from hook, now work in patt as given from * on 5th patt row (12[12:13] patt reps), turn.

Cont in patt for a further 10[10:15] cm ending with a 4th (WS) patt row, break yarn, turn.

Next row: Sk 5[6:7] patt reps and rejoin yarn to first dc of next rep. Starting with a 5th patt row, cont on these 7[6:6] patt reps only for a further 5 cm, ending with a 4th (WS) pattern row. Place a marker on one short edge to indicate the underarm then cont for a futher 5 cm, ending with a 4th (WS) patt row. Do not turn. Ch 31[37:43], turn.

Next row: 1dc in 3rd ch from hook *ch 6, sk 4 sts, 2dc, rep from * to end (12[12:13] patt reps), turn.

Starting with a 2nd patt row, cont in patt for a further 10[10:15] cm, ending with a 4th (WS) patt row, break yarn, turn.

Next row: Sk 1 patt rep and rejoin yarn to first dc of next rep.** Starting with a 5th patt row, cont on these 11[11:12] patt reps only for a further 20[25:25] cm, ending with a 4th (WS) patt row.

Now repeat work from ** to **, then cont in patt for a further 10 cm, place marker for hood at neck edge, then cont in patt for a further 10[15:20] cm, fasten off.

Hood

Using 7.5 mm hook, rejoin yarn to WS at hood marker on the left front of jacket, ch 1 (counts as first dc), work 7dc along edge up to first corner, dc3tog in the corner. Work 8 dc along the shoulder edge, dc3tog in next corner (on back). Work 20[26:26] dc across back, dc3tog in next corner. Work 8dc along the next shoulder edge, dc3tog in next corner, then 8 dc along edge to last hood marker on right front; turn.

Work in patt on these 56[62:62] sts as foll:

Row 1: (RS) Ch 1 (counts as first dc) sk first st, 1dc into next st, *ch 6, sk 4 sts, 2dc, rep from * to end (9[10:10] patt reps), turn. Now cont in patt as given for the body until work measures 30[30:35] cm ending with a 4th (WS) row.

Shape top

1st size only:

**Next row: Patt across first 3 reps, ch 6, 1dc in next dc, insert hook into next dc, yrh, draw through lp, insert hook into 2nd ch of next ch lp, yrh draw through a lp, yrh, draw through all 3 lps on hook, turn.

Next row: Ch 3, 1dc in 6-ch lp, ch 2, *2tr, ch 2, 1dc in next 6-ch lp, ch 2, rep from * to last 2 dc, 2tr, turn.

Next row: Ch 2 (counts as 1 tr), sk first tr, 1tr in next tr, (ch 3, sl st in next dc, ch 3, 2tr) 3 times, ch 3, sl st in next dc, turn.

Next row: Ch 1, 1dc in next 3-ch lp, ch 2, *2dc, ch 4, rep from * to last 2 sts, 2dc, fasten off. **

Rejoin yarn to other side of work at outside edge and work from ** to ** to match first side.

2nd and 3rd sizes only:

**Next row: Patt across first 4 reps, ch 6, sl st into next dc, turn.

Next row: Ch 3, 1dc into 6-ch lp, ch 2, 2dc, *ch 2, 1dc into 6-ch lp, ch 2, 2tr, rep from * to end, turn.

Next row: Patt across first 3 reps, ch 3, sl st into next dc, turn.

Next row: Ch 3, 2dc, *ch 4, 2dc, rep from * to end, fasten off. **

Rejoin yarn to other side of work at outside edge and work from ** to ** to match first side.

Sleeves (make 2 the same)

Using 7.5 mm hook, ch 39[39:51], turn.

Work in patt as given for rows 1–3 of the body (6[6:8] patt reps).

**Row 4: Ch 1 (counts as first dc), 1dc into first tr, 1dc into next tr, *ch 4, 2dc, rep from * to end placing last dc into 2nd of 2ch at beg of previous row, work 1dc back into this same ch, turn.

Row 5: Ch 1 (counts as 1dc), 2dc, *ch 6, 2dc, rep from * to end, 1dc into 1-ch at beg of prev row, turn.

Row 6: Ch 2 (counts as 1 tr), 2tr, *ch 2, 1dc into 6-ch lp, ch 2, 2tr, rep from * to end, 1tr into 1-ch at beg of prev row, turn.

Row 7: Ch 2 (counts as 1tr), 2tr, *ch 3, sl st into next dc, ch 3, 2tr, rep from * to end, 1tr into top of 2-ch at beg of prev row, turn.

Row 8: Ch 1 (counts as 1dc), 1dc into first tr, 1dc into each of next 2 tr, * 4 ch, 1dc into each of next 2tr, rep from * to end, 2dc into top of 2-ch at beg of prev row, turn.

Row 9: Ch 1 (counts as 1dc), 3dc, *ch 6, 2dc, rep from * to end, 1dc into next dc, 1dc into 1-ch at beg of prev row, turn.

Row 10: Ch 2 (counts as 1tr), 3tr, *ch 2, 1dc into 6 ch lp, ch 2, 2tr, rep from * to end, 1tr into next dc, 1tr into 1-ch at beg of prev row, turn.

Row 11: Ch 2 (counts as 1tr), 3tr, *ch 3, sl st into next dc, ch 3, 2tr, rep from * to end, 1tr into next tr, 1tr into top of 2-ch at beg of prev row, turn.

Row 12: Ch 1 (counts as 1dc), 1dc into first tr, ch 2, sk 1tr, 2dc, *ch 4, 2dc, rep from * to end, ch 2, sk 1tr, 2dc into top of 2-ch at beg of prev row, turn.

Row 13: Ch 1 (counts as 1dc), 1dc, ch 2, 2dc, *ch 6, 2dc, rep from * to end, ch 2, 1dc into next dc, 1dc into 1-ch at beg of previous row, turn.

Row 14: Ch 2 (counts as 1tr), 1tr, ch 2, 2tr, *ch 2, 1dc into 6 ch lp, ch 2, 2tr, rep from * to end, ch 2, 1tr into next dc, 1tr into 1-ch at beg of prev row, turn.

Row 15: Ch 2 (counts as 1tr), 1tr, ch 2, 2tr, *ch 3, sl st into next dc, ch 3, 2tr, rep from * to end, ch 2, 1tr into next tr, 1tr into top of 2-ch at beg of prev row, turn.

Row 16: Ch 1 (counts as 1dc), 1dc, *ch 4, 2dc, rep from * to end, last dc into top of 2-ch at beg of prev row (8[8:10] patt reps), turn.**

Work in patt as for the body rows, 5, 2 and 3, then work in patt as for sleeve from ** to ** (10[10:12] patt reps).

2nd & 3rd sizes only:

Next row: Ch 1 (counts as 1dc), 2dc, *ch 6, 2dc, rep from * to end, working last dc into 1-ch at beg of prev row, 1dc into same st, turn.

Next row: Ch 2 (counts as 1tr), ch 1, 2tr, *ch 2, 1dc into 6 ch lp, ch 2, 2tr, rep from * to end, working last tr into top of 2-ch at beg of prev row, 1tr into same st, turn.

Next row: Ch 2 (counts as 1tr), 1tr into first tr, ch 1, 2tr, *ch 3, sl st into next dc, ch 3, 2tr, rep from * to last 2 sts, ch 1, 2tr into top of 2-ch at beg of prev row, turn.

Next row: Ch 1 (counts as 1 dc), 1dc into first tr, *ch 4, 2dc, rep from * to end, 2dc into top of 2-ch at beg of prev row (12[14] patt reps), turn.

All sizes:

Place marker at each end of the last row. Work one more patt rep ending with a 4th patt row, fasten off.

Sleeve Edges

Using 7.5 mm hook and working from RS, rejoin yarn to lower edge of work, ch 2 (counts as 1dc), 26[26:30] dc along edge, turn.

Work 2 more rows in dc, fasten off.

Edging

With RS of work facing and using 7.5 mm hook, rejoin yarn to a point 1 st away from hood marker on left front body. Ch 2 (counts as 1dc), work 6dc to first outside corner, work 3dc into corner, then work 44[44:50] dc along front edge to lower left corner (outside corner). Work 3dc into corner, then work 96[108:132] dc to lower right front corner (outside corner). Work 3dc into corner, work 44[44:50] dc to top right front corner (outside corner). Work 3dc into corner, work 7dc to within 1 st of hood marker. Now dc3tog into corner (inside corner), then work 56[56:64] dc around hood. Finish with dc3tog into rem inside corner, sl st to top of 2-ch at beg of edging, turn.

Next row: Ch 2 (counts as first dc), work dc all round edging, working 3dc into corner st of each outside corner, and dc3tog at each inside corner. End with sl st to top of 2-ch at beg of edging, turn.

Repeat this last row one more time, fasten off.

Work in all ends. Lightly steam the edges.

Making up

Block and lightly steam the sleeves; leave to dry. Pin sleeve seams RS together and over sew the seams from cuff to marker, using a tapestry needle threaded with a length of matching yarn, so that the seams lie flat. Pin sleeves into armholes, RS together, matching sleeve seams to armhole markers on body. Over sew the seams, using a tapestry needle threaded with a length of matching yarn.

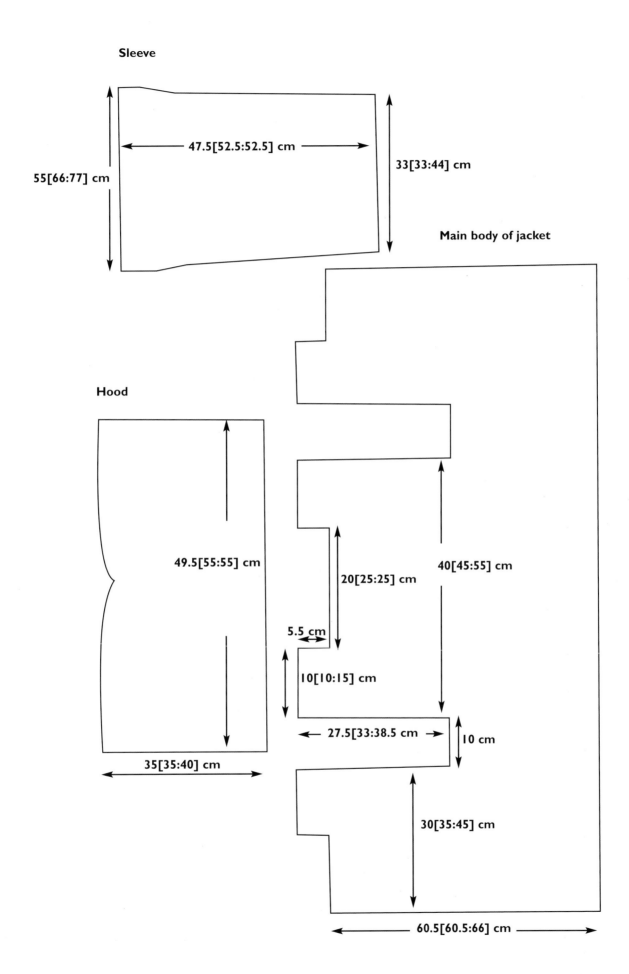

Sleeve

47.5[52.5:52.5] cm

55[66:77] cm

33[33:44] cm

Main body of jacket

Hood

49.5[55:55] cm

20[25:25] cm

40[45:55] cm

5.5 cm

10[10:15] cm

35[35:40] cm

27.5[33:38.5 cm

10 cm

30[35:45] cm

60.5[60.5:66] cm

part 6

CROCHET KIDS

Garden flower dress

This bobbly bodice has a simple skirt made from a light Tana Lawn print cotton. The yarn is easy to work with and to wash and care for – always a consideration with children's clothes.

YOU WILL NEED:

- GGH Samoa, 50% cotton, 50% acrylic (95 m per 50 g ball), 2 [2–3, 3–4] × 50 g balls in Aqua (col A), 1 × 50 g ball in Hot Pink (col B)
- 5 mm and 4 mm hook
- 75 cm light cotton fabric, 114 cm wide, and matching sewing thread
- Vintage buttons
- Tapestry needle
- Sewing machine or needle

Tension

16 stitches and 10 rows = 10 cm using 5 mm hook over bobble patt.

Sizes

18 months–2 yr [2–3 yr:3–4 yr].

Measurements

Chest size: 48[51:56] cm.

Making a bobble

To make a bobble (bo) for this pattern, *yrh, insert hook in st, yrh and draw the yarn through, yrh and draw through 2 lps only. Repeat from * 4 more times, inserting the hook through the same stitch every time (6 lps on the hook). Yrh and draw yarn through all loops to make 1 bobble (1bo).

Back bodice

Using 5 mm hook and col A, ch 40[44:48], turn.

Row 1: 1tr in 3rd ch from hook, tr to end (39[43:47] sts), turn.

Row 2: Ch 1, 2dc, *1bo in next st, 3dc, rep from * to end, turn.

Row 3: Ch 2, tr to end, turn.

Rows 2 & 3 form the pattern; cont in this way until 10 rows of patt worked.

Shape armholes

Row 11: Sl st over first 3 sts, then tr to end, turn.

Row 12: Sl st over first 3 sts, *1bo in next st, 3dc, rep from * to end, turn.

Shoulder straps

Row 13: Ch 2, 8[12:16]tr, turn.

Cont in patt on these 9[13:17] sts for a further 8 rows, fasten off.

Rejoin yarn 9[13:17] sts in from opposite armhole edge and cont in patt for 9 rows, starting with a tr row, fasten off.

Front bodice

Work as for back bodice but make shoulder straps only 4 rows deep, fasten off.

Epaulettes

Take the back bodice and join col B to the outside edge of the left shoulder strap. With WS facing and 4 mm hook, work dc across the edge of the strap (9[13:17] sts), turn.

Next row: (Shell patt) ch 1, sk 1, *5tr in next st, sk 1, rep from * to last st, 1dc, fasten off.

Rejoin col B to the inside edge of the right shoulder strap. With WS facing, work dc across the strap edge, as for the left strap. Turn and work a row of shell patt, as for the left strap, fasten off.

Bodice trim

Join col B to the right-hand edge of the bottom of the back bodice. With WS facing, work dc across the bottom edge (39[43:47] sts), turn.

Next row: (Shell patt) ch 1, sk 1, *5tr in next st, sk 1, rep from * to last st, 1dc, fasten off.

Rejoin col B to the left-hand edge of the bottom of the back bodice. With WS facing, work dc across the bottom edge, as for the back-bodice trim. Turn and work a row of shell patt as for the back bodice, fasten off.

Finishing

Thread a tapestry needle with a length of col A and stitch the front and back bodice pieces together at the side seams, working on the WS. Turn the bodice to the RS and join the shoulders so that the epaulettes overlap the front straps. Sew in place, concealing your stitches within your crochet work. Stitch buttons on to the epaulettes to finish.

Skirt

Cut a piece of fabric 100 x 65 [105 x 68:110 x 72] cm, allowing for one seam at back of garment. Turn under one long edge of the fabric by 5 mm; pin and press. Turn under by another 1.5 cm; pin and press. Hand or machine stitch along the edge, to hem. Finish the raw edges of the fabric with machine zigzag stitch. Bring the two short edges of the fabric RS together, pin and then machine stitch the seam, taking a 1.5 cm allowance. Work two rows of tacking stitches around the zigzag-stitched top edge of the fabric, leaving long ends of tacking thread at either end of your stitching. Pull on these long threads to draw the tacking thread up and gather the edge of the fabric. Pin the gathered edge to the bottom of the bodice, so the RS are together and matching the back seam of the skirt to the centre back of the bodice. Adjust the gathers so that the skirt falls nicely and then tack in place. Hand sew in place, stitching along the place where the shell pattern trim joins the bodice. Press lightly, and turn to RS.

YOU WILL NEED:

- Blue Sky Alpaca 100% alpaca (100 m per 50 g skein), 2 x 50 g balls in Turquoise shade 307 (col A), 1 x 50 g ball in Vivid Lilac shade 50 (col B)
- 3.5 mm and 4 mm hooks

Tension
Scarf: 22htr and 14 rows = 10 cm square.
Hat: 17dc and 24 rows = 10 cm square.

Finished measurements
Scarf: 68 cm long and 9 cm wide.
Hat: 40 cm diameter at its widest point.

Note
Yarn amounts are based on average requirements and are approximate.

pixie hat and scarf

This cute matching set will keep any babe snug and warm. The elfin hat with its pointed top is edged with crab stitch in a contrasting colour, and the scarf has a tassel border.

Scarf

Using col A and 4 mm hook, ch 130, turn.
Row 1: 1htr in 2nd chain from hook, htr to end (130 sts), turn.
Row 2: Ch 2, sk first st, work htr in front lp of each st to end, turn.
Row 3: Ch 2, sk first st, work htr in back lp of each st to end, turn.
Rep last 2 rows, 5 more times.
Next row: Ch 1, work dc in front lp of each st to end, finish off.

Fringing

Cut several lengths of col B, each 15 cm long. Take 6 lengths and bunch together. Fold the bunch in half. Insert the 4 mm hook in a gap between rows on one short edge. Pick up the folded bunch of yarn and draw through the scarf; don't pull through. Pass the loose ends of the bunch of yarn through the loop and then pull to secure the bunch tightly. Continue in the same way along the rest of the edge and along the opposite edge.

Hat

Using col A and 3.5 mm hook, ch 4, join with sl st to make ring.
Rnd 1: Ch 1, 5dc into ring, join with sl st to top of 1-ch.
Rnd 2 and every alternate even rnd up to rnd 12: Ch 1, dc into each st, join with a sl st to top of 1-ch.
Rnd 3: Ch 1, 2dc into next st, *1dc, 2dc into next st, rep from * to end, join with sl st to top of 1-ch (9 sts).

Rnd 5: Ch 1, 1dc, 2dc into next st, *2dc, 2dc into next st, rep from * to end, join with sl st to top of 1-ch (12 sts).

Rnd 7: Ch 1, 2dc in next st, *1dc, 2dc in next st, rep from * to end, join with sl st to top of 1-ch (18 sts).

Rnd 9: Ch 1, 1dc, 2dc into next st, *2dc, 2dc into next st, rep from * to end, join with sl st to top of 1-ch (24 sts).

Rnd 11: Ch 1, 1dc, 2dc into next st, *2dc, 2dc into next st, rep from * to end, join with sl st to top of 1-ch (32 sts).

Rnd 13: Ch 1, 2dc, 2dc into next st, *3dc, 2dc into next st, rep from * to end, join with sl st to top of 1-ch (40 sts).

Rnd 14: Ch 1, 2dc, 2dc into next st, *3dc, 2dc into next st, rep from * to end, join with sl st to top of 1-ch (50 sts). Change to 4 mm hook.

Rnd 15: As rnd 2.

Rnd 16: Ch 1, 3dc, 2dc into next st, *4dc, 2dc into next st, rep from * to end, join with sl st to top of 1-ch (60 sts).

Rnd 17: As rnd 2.

Rnd 18: Ch 1, 4dc, 2dc into next st, *5dc, 2dc into next st, rep from * to end, join with sl st to top of 1-ch (70 sts).

Rnd 19: As rnd 2.

Rnd 20: Ch 1, 5dc, 2dc into next st, *6dc, 2dc into next st, rep from * to last 6 sts, 6dc, join with sl st to top of 1-ch (78 sts).

Rep rnd 2, working straight until the hat measures 19 cm from top; fasten off.

Earflaps (make 2 the same)

Using col A and 3.5 mm hook, ch 5, turn.

Row 1: 1dc into 2nd ch from hook, 2dc, 3dc into last ch. Then work along the other side of the foundation ch without turning the work, 1dc into each st, ch 1, turn.

Row 2: 3dc, (2dc into next st) 3 times, 3dc, ch 1, turn.

Row 3: 4dc, (2dc into next st, 1dc) twice, 2dc into next st, 3dc, turn.

Row 4: 5dc, (2dc into next st) 6 times, 4dc, ch 1, turn.

Row 5: 6dc, 2dc into next st, 3dc into next 3dc, 2dc into next dc, 7dc to end, ch 1, turn.

Row 6: 8dc, 2dc into next st, 4dc, 2dc into next st, 6dc to end, fasten off, leaving a long loose end of yarn for sewing up.

Edgings

Using col B and 3.5 mm hook, join yarn to edge of hat at back seam, with RS facing. Ch 1, then work dc all around the edge of the hat and earflaps, join with a sl st to 1-ch. Ch 1, then work dc backwards (crab stitch), working the sts slightly looser over the earflaps to maintain the shape. Take your time, as crab stitch is quite fiddly, but worth it for the effect it produces.

Making up

Place a marker 11 ch to the left of the back seam on the hat. Match the right top corner of one earflap to this marker and then pin the earflap to the edge of the hat, stretching it slightly to cover 11 sts, sew in place. Repeat, placing a second marker 11 ch to the right of the back seam and matching it to the left top corner of the remaining earflap. Work in any loose ends.

baby play mat

This lovely soft cotton is gentle on baby skin. The tension isn't crucial here, though it is best to make sure that the holes are not large enough to snag little fingers and toes. This is a great gift for a new baby, and for using up oddments of cotton. Try to use the same thicknesses of yarns to keep the edges even.

Method

Using any col and 4.5 mm hook, ch 68, turn.

Row 1: 1dc into 2nd ch from hook, dc to end (68 sts), turn.

Row 2: Ch 1, dc in back lp of each st to end, changing to new col on last st, turn.

Rep row 2 until work measures 60 cm, changing col as liked every 2 rows, fasten off.

Using any col, join yarn to any point on edge of blanket, RS facing, and work dc all round edge. Work 3dc into each corner. Work in any loose ends.

Tip

This blanket was made using nine different colours. You can choose to use a variety of different bright colours and combine them in contrasting bands, or use the same colour in a number of different shades to get the same, multi-hued effect.

YOU WILL NEED:

- Rowan Handknit Cotton 100% cotton (approx 85 m per 50 g ball), 1 x 50 g ball each of Gooseberry 219, Linen 205, Mango Fool 319, Diana 287, Decadent 314, Lupin 305, Spanish Red 307, Sugar 303 and Fruit Salad 203
- 4.5 mm hook

Tension
Not crucial.

Finished Measurements
48 x 61 cm.

afghan cot blanket

A crocheted cover in cotton stays cool in the summer months. This blanket is the ideal size for a Moses basket or a pram. The patches are so quick, easy and fun to make that you could get quite carried away and stitch up a bed-sized quilt before you know it.

YOU WILL NEED:

- Rowan DK cotton, 100% cotton (84 m per 50 g ball), 3 x 50 g balls in Bleached 263 (col A), 4 x 50 g balls in Sunflower 304 (col B), 7 x 50 g balls in Sugar 303 (col C)
- 3.5 mm hook
- Tapestry needle

Tension
Each patch measures 11 cm at the widest point.

Finished size
87 x 68 cm.

Patch (make 54)

Using col A and 3.5 mm hook, ch 5, join with a sl st to make ring.
Rnd 1: Ch 3, 1tr in ring, (ch 1, 2tr in ring) 5 times, ch 1, join with sl st to top of 3-ch, fasten off.
Rnd 2: Join col B to any 1-ch sp, ch 3, (1tr, ch 1, 2tr) into same ch sp, ch 1, *(2tr, ch 1, 2tr) into next ch sp, ch 1, rep from * 4 times, join with sl st to top of 3-ch, fasten off.
Rnd 3: Join in col C to a 1-ch sp at any corner of the hexagon, ch 3, (1tr, ch 1, 2tr) into same space, ch 1, 2tr in next ch sp, *(2tr, ch 1, 2tr) into next ch sp, ch 1, 2tr in next ch sp, ch 1, rep from * 4 times, join with a sl st to top of 3-ch.
Rnd 4: Ch 1, 1dc in each st except at corners, where 2dc in each corner st, join with sl st to 1-ch; break off yarn leaving a length of about 30 cm for joining patches.

Half-patch (make 9)

Using col A and 3.5 mm hook, ch 5, join with a sl st to make ring.
Row 1: Ch 3, 1tr in ring, (ch 1, 2tr in ring) twice, fasten off.
Row 2: Join col B to top of 3-ch, ch 3, 1tr into same st, *ch 1, (2tr, ch 1, 2tr) in next ch sp, rep from * once, ch 1, 2tr into last st, fasten off.
Row 3: Join in col C to top of 3-ch, ch 3, 1tr into same st, *ch 1, 2tr into ch sp, ch 1, (2tr, ch 1, 2tr) into corner sp, rep from * once, ch 1, 2tr into ch sp, ch 1, 2tr into last st, fasten off, turn.
Row 4: Rejoin col C to top of 3-ch; 1ch, 1dc in each st except at the two corners, where 2dc in each corner st; break yarn, leaving a length about 30 cm for joining patches.

Making up

Stitch the patches together so that you have a blanket made up of nine rows of six and a half patches. Alternate which end of the row the half-patches fall on, so that the finished blanket has two long straight sides and two short zigzag-edge ends. Use the 30-cm tails to join the patches together.

Join col C to one corner at the beginning of a straight edge, ch 1, work dc along this edge, then work 3dc into the corner. Work dc along the zigzag edge, working 3dc into the outer corners and skipping two sts at the inner corners. Work the other straight edge and zigzag edge in the same way. Work another round of dc in col C, then two rounds in col A, two rounds in col B, and finish with two more rounds of col C.

1 Hold the patches right-sides together and use whipstitch to join them using the tail ends of the yarn.

2 When joining the patches together, work out from one corner, creating a zigzag edge along one side (the short end of the blanket), and a straight edge along the other (long side of the blanket).

crochet dolls

These two little dolls can be given any character you choose. The instructions are for a doll with contrasting feet and hands. Change the colours, or design a different set of clothes for the dolls using the patterns provided as a base.

Legs

Using col B and 3 mm hook, ch 4, join with sl st to form a ring.

Rnd 1: Ch 1, 9dc in ring, join with sl st to 1-ch at beg of rnd.

Rnd 2: Ch 1, 1dc in first st, *2dc in next st, rep from * to end, join with sl st to 1-ch at beg of rnd (20 sts).

Rnd 3: Ch 1 (counts as first dc), 19dc, join with sl st to top of 1-ch at beg of rnd.

Rep last rnd 5 more times, changing to col A in last sl st of last rnd, break off col B.

Rep 3rd rnd 18 more times, fasten off.

Work a second leg in the same way but do not fasten off at end.

Body

With hook still in last st of the second leg, insert it into last st of first leg; pull yarn through and then through st on hook to work 1 sl st. Ch 1, then work dc round top of first leg and then round top of 2nd leg, join with sl st to top of 1-ch (40 sts). Work 15 rnds of dc on these sts.

Next row: (front chest) Ch 1, 19dc (20 sts), turn.

Work 8 rows of dc on these sts, fasten off.

Rejoin yarn to unworked sts and then work 8 rows of dc on these 20 sts (back chest), do not fasten off.

Arms

Insert hook in last st of front chest and pull yarn through. Pull through loop on hook to make sl st. Ch 1, then work 17dc round armhole edge, join with sl st to 1-ch (18 sts).

Next rnd: Ch 1, 17dc, join with sl st to 1-ch.

Rep last rnd 11 more times, changing to col B in last sl st of last rnd, break off col A. Work 6 more rounds of dc.

Next rnd: Ch 1, sk 1 st, *1dc in next st, sk 1 st, rep from * 7 more times, join with sl st to 1-ch (9 sts), fasten off.

Join col A to top of other armhole opening, using a sl st to join front and back together. Then work as for first arm.

YOU WILL NEED:

- Rowan 4-ply Cotton 100% cotton (170 m per 50 g ball), 1 x 50 g ball in 119 Allure or 121 Ripple (col A), 1 x 50 g ball in 130 Ardour (col B), and oddments of 133 Cheeky, 129 Aegean, 132 Bloom, and 115 Nightsky (you will need three different colours to make the clothes and hair)
- 3 mm hook
- Polyester fibrefill stuffing
- Tapestry needle

Notes

After the legs have been made separately, the body is worked in one piece, with no seams (see tip on page 150).

A single ball of Rowan 4-ply cotton is more than enough to make a whole doll. The clothes and hair each take a fraction of a ball so this is a good project for using up any yarn left over from another project.

Finished size: 35 cm high.

Neck and head

Rejoin col A at neck edge, ch 1, work 33dc round neck edge, join with sl st to 1-ch.

Rnd 1: Ch 1, 33dc, join with sl st to 1-ch (34 sts).

Rnd 2: Ch 1, sk 1 st, *1dc in next st, sk 1 st, rep from * to end, join with sl st to 1-ch (17 sts).

Rnd 3: Ch 1, 16dc, join with sl st to 1-ch.

Rnd 4: Ch 1, 1dc in first st, *2dc in next st, rep from * to end (34 sts).

Rep rnd 1 for 13 more times, do not break yarn.

Tip

Though you start by making two separate legs, these are joined and the body is worked upwards from there. The rest of the doll is constructed in one piece and you do not have to stitch any seams. You may find it easier to stuff the doll as you go rather than waiting until you reach the top of the head. When the doll is completed, simply darn in any stray ends.

Dress or top

Bodice back

Using your chosen colour and 4 mm hook, ch 16, turn.

Row 1: 1dc in 2nd ch from hook, dc to end (16 sts), turn.

Row 2: Ch 1 (counts as first dc), 15dc, turn.

Rep last row 2 more times.

Row 5: (Shoulder strap) ch 1, 3dc, turn.

Rep last row 9 times, fasten off.

Rejoin yarn to edge of bodice and work 2nd shoulder strap; do not fasten off at end, turn.

Next row: (Bodice front) ch 1, 3dc, ch 8, 4dc along edge of first shoulder strap, turn.

Next row: Ch 1, 15dc, turn.

Rep last row 2 more times.

Next rnd: Ch 1, 15dc, ch 6, sl st to bodice back, 16dc, ch 6, sl st to bodice front (44 sts).

Next rnd: Ch 1, 43dc, join with sl st to 1-ch.

Next rnd: Ch 1, 1dc in next st, *2 dc in next st, 1 dc in next st, repeat from * to end; join with sl st to 1-ch (55 sts).

Next rnd: Ch 1, 54dc, join with sl st to 1-ch.

Rep the last rnd 19 more times for a dress or 6 more times for a top.

Last rnd: (picot edge) *ch 4, sl st to base of 4-ch, 4dc, rep from * to end, fasten off.

Knickers

Using your chosen colour and 4 mm hook, ch 44, join with sl st to form ring.

Rnd 1: Ch 1, 43dc, join with sl st to 1-ch.

Rnd 2: (Eyelets) ch 1, 1dc in next st, ch 2, skip 2 sts, *2dc, ch 2, skip 2 sts, rep from * to end, join with sl st to 1-ch.

Rep first rnd 10 more times.

Next rnd: (Divide for legs) ch 1, 21dc, join with sl st to 1-ch (22 sts).

Work 2 rounds of dc on these 22sts, fasten off.

Rejoin yarn at base of 1-ch on first rnd of first knicker leg. Work 2nd leg in same way.

Making up

Stuff the doll with polyester fibrefill stuffing, but not too firmly. Press the opening at the top of the head together with your fingers and work sl st across the opening to close; fasten off yarn.

Eyes

Sew on buttons for eyes. Alternatively, if this little character doll is intended as a gift for a very small child, then use embroidery, or appliqué circles of fabric onto the face for the eyes. Buttons could prove a choking hazard.

Hair

Cut short lengths of yarn. Taking 3 strands at a time, fold in half and use the crochet hook to pull the fold through one of the sl sts at the top of the head. Hook the ends through this loop and pull tightly to knot. Repeat to draw 3 strands of yarn through each sl st at the top of the head. Trim the ends of the hair neatly.

Increasing and decreasing

Crochet is very versatile because you can create complex shapes. It is much easier to crochet a circle, for example, than to knit one. Shaping pieces of work involves increasing and decreasing stitches. To increase, you usually have to work more than one stitch in the top of a stitch on the previous row; to decrease, you usually have to skip a stitch. In this project, increases and decreases are used to taper the ends of the arms and legs and to shape the neck, and to make the dress slightly flared.

Red cabled suit

Cables in crochet are unusual, but look very effective. This warm yarn stitches up an extra cosy suit for a small baby. Buttons at the shoulder and an elasticated waistline make for easy dressing.

YOU WILL NEED:

- Debbie Bliss Baby Cashmerino 55% merino wool, 33% microfibre, 12% cashmere (125 m per 50 g ball), 4[5:6] x 50 g balls in Red 700
- 3.5 mm hook
- Waist length of narrow elastic for trousers
- Tapestry needle
- Two 1 cm buttons

Note
Yarn amounts given are based on average requirements and are approximate.

Tension
19 sts and 10 rows = 10 cm using 3.5 mm hook over dc.

Sizes
Newborn–3 months: [6–9 months:12–18 months].

Finished measurements
Sweater chest: 41[46:51] cm.

Pattern notes

Elastic rib pattern
To work 1x1 rib for the sweater welt, work thus:

Foundation row: Ch 3 (counts as first tr), *1tr around front stem of next tr, 1tr around back stem of next tr, rep from * to end.

Pattern row: Ch 3 (counts as first tr), *1tr around stem of each tr – if st is at front then go round front stem, if at back, then around back stem to give 1x1 rib line. This last row is rep throughout.

Cable panel (chart on page 157)
Work cable panel from chart throughout, commencing with WS (first) row of chart.

1trf = 1tr around front stem of next tr

1trb = 1tr around back stem of next tr

Left lean cable = Skip next 2tr, 1dtr round front stem of each of next 2 tr, taking hook in front of dtr just worked, return to unworked tr farthest from hook and work 1dtr round front stem of the two unworked tr.

Right lean cable = Skip next 2tr, 1dtr round front stem of each of next 2 tr, taking hook behind dtr just worked, return to unworked tr farthest from hook and work 1dtr round front stem of the two unworked dc.

Trousers (work 2 legs alike)

Cuff
Using 4 mm hook, ch 27[29:31], turn.

Row 1: 1dc in 3rd ch from hook, dc to end (26[28:30] sts), turn.

Row 2: Ch 1 (counts as first dc), dc to end, turn.

Rep last row until cuff measures 3 cm.

Next (inc) row: Ch 1 (counts as first dc), dc to end and inc 8[10:14] sts evenly along the row at same time (34[38:44] sts), turn.

Leg
Next row: Ch 2 (counts as first tr), tr to end, turn.

Rep prev row, inc 1 st at each end of next and every foll alt row until 58[62:68] sts. Work straight until leg measures 20[23:28] cm, turn.

Shape crutch
Next row: Sl st over first 4 sts, tr to last 4 sts, turn.

Next row: Sl st over first 2 sts, tr to last 2 sts, turn.

Cont in tr, dec 1 st at each end of next 2[2:3] rows until 42[46:50] sts. Work straight until crutch measures 11[12.5:14] cm, turn.

Shape top
Next row: Ch 2 (counts as first tr), 20[22:24]tr (21[23:25] sts), turn.

Next row: Ch 2 (counts as first tr), 9[11:11]tr (10[12:12] sts), turn.

Next row: Ch 2 (counts as first tr), tr to end, fasten off.

Take the two leg pieces and match up the lower points of the crutch seams; pin along centre front crutch seam. Using a tapestry needle and length of matching yarn, stitch the seam on the WS. With RS facing, rejoin yarn to top edge and work 6 rows dc across the top, fasten off.

Making up trousers

Using a tapestry needle and length of matching yarn, and working on WS, stitch centre back crutch seam and then inside leg seams. Fold the waistband (the section worked in dc) to WS and sl st around, leaving a small opening at the back. Insert elastic, adjust to fit and fasten off securely. Stitch the waistband opening closed and give the trousers a very light steam.

Sweater

Back

Ch 44[48:52], turn.

Row 1: 1dtr in 4th ch from hook, dtr to end (42[46:50] sts), turn.

Cont in 1x1 rib (see elastic rib pattern on page 154) until work measures 4 cm.

Next row: Ch 2 (counts as first tr), tr to end, turn.

Rep prev row until back measures 14[16:17.5] cm, turn.

Shape armholes

Next row: Sl st over 2 sts, dc to last 2 sts (38[42:46]sts), turn.

Cont in dc, dec 1 st at each end of next 2 rows until 34[38:42] sts. Work straight until armhole measures 9.5[10.5:12] cm, turn.

Shape shoulder

Row 1: Ch 1 (counts as first dc), 8[9:10] dc (9[10:11] sts), turn.

Continue on these sts only and work 2 more rows in dc, turn.

Buttonhole

Next row: Ch 1 3[3:4] dc, ch 2, sk 2 dc, dc to end.

Next row: Ch 1 (counts as first dc), 2[3:3] dc, 3dc in 2-ch lp, dc to end, turn.

Work 2 more rows in dc, fasten off.

Rejoin yarn 9[10:11] sts from edge of other armhole, dc to end. Work as first shoulder, reversing position of buttonhole.

Front

Ch 45[47:53], turn.

Row 1: 1dtr in 4th ch from hook, dtr to end (43[47:51] sts), turn.

Cont in 1x1 rib (see elastic rib pattern on page 154) until work measures 4 cm.

Next row: Ch 2 (counts as first tr), tr to end, turn.

Start and work cable panel from diagram over centre 21 sts thus:

Ch 2 (counts as first tr), 10[12:14] tr, work 21 st from cable panel (see page 157), 11[13:15] tr, turn.

Cont working panel with plain tr each side throughout and at the same time, work until back measures 14[16:17.5] cm.

Shape armholes

Next row: Sl st over 2 sts, work to last 2 sts (39[43:47] sts), turn.

Cont working in patt, dec 1 st at each end of next 2 rows until 35[39:43] sts. Work straight until armhole measures 6[7.5:8.5] cm ending with WS row, turn.

Shape neck and shoulder

Next row: Ch 2 (counts as first tr), work in patt over 13[14:15] sts (14[15:16] sts), turn.

Cont working in patt over these sts only for first side, dec 1 st at neck edge on next 5 rows (9[10:11] sts). Work straight until armhole measures (9.5[10.5:12] cm), turn.

Next row: Ch 1 (counts as first dc), dc to end, turn.

Rep last row once, fasten off.

With RS facing, rejoin yarn 14[15:16] sts from edge of other armhole. Work to shape neck and shoulder as for first side reversing shaping.

Front neckband

With RS facing rejoin yarn to neck edge and work 3 rows dc, dec 5 sts evenly along last of these rows, fasten off.

Back neckband

Work as for front neckband but only dec 3 sts on last row.

Cable panel chart

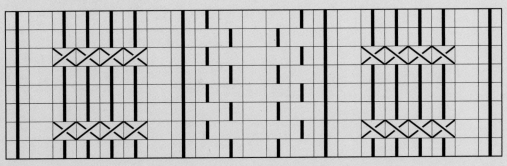

Key

Each square = 1st (tr) and 1 row

| | RS row 1trf, WS row 1trb

⊠ Left lean cable

⊠ Right lean cable

21 sts x 4 rows repeat

For a guide to abbreviations, see pattern notes on page 154.

Sleeves

Cuff

Ch 21[23:26], turn.

Row 1: 1dtr in 4th ch from hook, dtr to end (19[21:24] sts), turn.

Cont in 1x1 rib (see elastic rib pattern on page 154) until work measures 2 cm.

Next row: Ch 2 (counts as first tr), tr to end, turn.

Cont working in tr, inc 1 st at each end of next and every foll alt [3rd:3rd] row until 35[39:42] sts. Work straight until sleeve measures 13[15:18.5] cm, turn.

Shape top

Next row: Sl st over first 2 sts, tr to last 2 sts, turn.

Rep last row once more (27[31:34] sts), turn. Cont in tr, dec 1 st at each end of each row until 17[19:22] sts remain. Dec 4 sts evenly over next row, fasten off.

Making up

Overlap the back shoulders over the front. Use a tapestry needle and length of matching yarn to slip stitch at shoulder edge. Sew on buttons to correspond with buttonholes. Working on WS, set in sleeves and stitch the seams round the armholes. Stitch the side and sleeve seams. Give the sweater a very light steam.

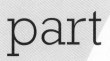

FUN ACCESSORIES

magic shopping bag

This handy holdall scrunches up small to fit in your handbag. But when you get to the greengrocer's, it will expand to accommodate all your fruit and veg. Of course, you could choose to use it to transport wet towels from the beach or pool, or to store stuff in at home. And if you choose to make it from the bright pink mason line suggested here, you will be able to spot it from a long way away.

Bag

Using the mason line or hemp and 4 mm hook, ch 6, join with sl st to form ring.

Rnd 1: Ch 3, 11 tr into ring, join with sl st to top of 3ch.

Rnd 2: Ch 4, 1 tr into next st, *ch 1, 1 tr into next st, rep from * to end, join with sl st to 3rd ch of the 4-ch.

Rnd 3: Sl st into next ch from hook, ch 5, 1 tr into next ch sp, *ch 2, 1 tr into next ch sp, rep from * to end, ch 2, join with a sl st to 3rd ch of the 5-ch.

Rnd 4: Sl st into next ch from hook, ch 5, 1 tr into first ch sp, *ch 2, 1 tr into next ch sp, ch 2, (1 tr, ch 2, 1 tr) into next ch sp; rep from * to last ch sp, ch 2, 1 tr into that sp, ch 2, join with sl st to 3rd ch of the 5-ch.

Rnd 5: Sl st into next ch from hook, ch 6, 1 tr into next ch sp, *ch 3, 1 tr into next ch sp, rep from * to end, ch 3, join with sl st to 3rd ch of the 6-ch.

Rnd 6: Sl st into next ch from hook, ch 7, 1 tr into next ch sp, *ch 4, 1 tr into next ch sp, rep from * to end, ch 4, join with sl st to 3rd ch of the 7-ch.

Rnd 7: Sl st into next ch from hook, ch 7, 1 tr into first ch sp, *ch 4, (1 tr, ch 4, 1 tr) into next ch sp, rep from * to end, ch 4, join with sl st to 3rd ch of the 7-ch.

Rnd 8: Sl st into next ch from hook, ch 8, 1 tr into next ch sp, *ch 5, 1 tr into next ch sp, rep from * to end, ch 5, join with sl st to 3rd ch of the 8-ch.

Tie a short length of contrasting yarn to the last 5-ch, this acts as a marker to help you when counting rounds. Rep the last rnd 15 times, do not fasten off.

Border and handles

Next rnd: Work sl st into each of the sts round the top edge of the bag (there should be about 210 sts, but don't worry if you are one or two out).

Next rnd: Ch 80 (to form first handle), sk 50, sl st in next st, then work 53 dc, ch 80 (to form 2nd handle), sk 50, dc to end, join with sl st to base of first handle.

Next rnd: Work a round of dc, join with sl st to first dc, fasten off.

YOU WILL NEED:

- 2 x 70 m reels of #18 mason line (pink), or 3 hanks of House of Hemp DK Expressions hand-coloured hemp in Gosh (turquoise)
- 4 mm hook

Tension
Not crucial and will vary with yarn used.

Finished measurements
Approximately 50 cm wide and 45 cm long, excluding handles.

The tricky bit

After completing round 8, tie a marker to the last 5-ch. The nature of this bag makes it hard to distinguish between the different rounds. Marking the 8th round will make it easier to count up how many rounds have been completed.

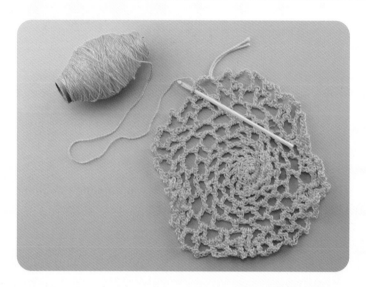

Tip

You are not limited in the types of yarns you can use for crochet. You can use any type of yarn you like – even string, as in this project, or wire, strips of fabric and ribbon. Having said this, some yarns are easier to work with than others. The best yarns of all are those that are smooth and even, and tightly twisted. With loosely twisted yarns, the hook has a tendency to slip between the fibres, as with the hemp used to make the turquoise bag. With textured yarns, it is also more difficult to obtain an even tension. Experiment and practise with the more unusual yarns to discover their potential.

YOU WILL NEED:

- Rowan Big Wool 100% wool (80 m per 100 g ball), 2 × 100 g balls in White Hot 001 (col A)
- Debbie Bliss Cashmerino Superchunky 55% merino wool, 33% microfibre, 12% cashmere (75 m per 50g ball), 1 × 50 g ball in Blue 006 (col B)
- 9 mm and 6 mm hooks

Tension

10 st and 8 rows = 10 cm using 6 mm hook.

Special abbreviations

Fur st = fur stitch.
Puff = puff stitch.

snow bonnet

Come rain or snow, this fluffy fur-stitch bonnet will keep your ears warm while keeping your image cool. The fur-stitch trim looks more complicated than it is, and the pom-poms are just oversized versions of the kind that you made at school.

Fur stitch

Hold the yarn so it passes up and over the first and second fingers of left hand, and is then held lightly between the second and third fingers. Insert the hook into the next stitch and extend the yarn to required length by raising the second finger. Keeping the hook to the right of the yarn, use the hook to pick up the yarn lying between the 2nd and 3rd fingers and draw a loop through the stitch (2 loops on hook). Then, keeping the hook to the left of the yarn over the fingers, use the hook to pick up the working yarn and draw it through both loops on hook. Remove the fingers from the loop to make 1 fur st.

Puff stitch

*Yrh, insert hook into next st, yrh and draw large loop through very loosely. * Rep from * to * 4 more times into same stitch (11 loops on hook). Yrh and pull through 10 loops (2 loops on hook). Yrh and pull through remaining loops to make 1 puff.

Trim

Using col A and 9 mm hook, ch 38, turn.
Row 1: 1dc into 3rd ch from hook, dc to end (37 sts), turn.
Row 2: Ch 1 (counts as first dc), 35 fur st, 1dc, turn.
Row 3: Ch 1 (counts as first dc), dc to end, turn.
Row 4: As row 2.
Row 5: As row 3.
Row 6: As row 2, fasten off.

Main body

Turn work upside down but with same side facing, and join col B to edge of foundation ch, using a 6 mm hook.
Row 7: Ch 2 (counts as first htr), htr to end (37 sts), turn.
Row 8: As row 7.
Row 9: Ch 3 (counts as first tr), *1 puff, 1tr, rep from * to end, turn.
Row 10: As row 7.
Row 11: As row 9.
Row 12: As row 7, fasten off.

Row 13: Rejoin yarn to 13th st from end, ch 2 (counts as first htr), 12htr (13 sts), turn.

Cont in htr on these 13 sts for 10 rows; fasten off.

Making up

Lay your work out flat, WS up, so the flap (worked in htr) is at the top. Bring the left-hand side edge of the flap to meet the edge formed by those unworked stitches of row 12 to the left of the flap. Pin so the RS are together and then sew up, using a tapestry needle and length of col B. Repeat on the right-hand side of the flap to form the bonnet shape.

Use col A to make two pom-poms, each approximately 8 cm in diameter (see page 75). To make a tie, use col B and a 6 mm hook to ch 45. Use sl st to attach the tie to one of the bottom corners at the front of the bonnet; fasten off the end securely. Attach a pom-pom to the other end of the tie. Repeat to make another tie for the other corner.

YOU WILL NEED:

For the short-length cuffs:
Rowan Wool Cotton 50% merino wool, 50% cotton (113 m per 50 g ball), 1 x 50 g ball each of Grey 903 (col A) and Lilac 954 (col B)

For the long-length cuffs:
Rowan Wool Cotton 50% merino wool, 50% cotton (113 m per 50 g ball), 2 x 50 g balls in Lilac 954 (col B), 1 x 50 g ball in Beige 930 (col C)

- 3.5 mm hook
- Tapestry needle
- Approximately 10 buttons for decoration

Tension
7 x 4 shells = 10 cm.

cuffs

These fashionable cuffs will fill the gap between your sleeve and hand, as well as the gap in your wardrobe. You can make two lengths, short or long, and decorate them with surface chain embellishments and tiny pearl buttons.

Short-length cuffs (make 2)

Using col A and 3.5 mm hook, ch 45, turn.

Row 1: 2tr into 3rd ch from hook, sk 2 ch, 1dc, *sk 2 ch, 5tr into next ch, sk 2 ch, 1dc, rep from * to last 3ch, 3tr into last ch, turn.

Row 2: Ch 1, *5tr into next dc, 1dc into centre of shell, rep from * to end, turn.

Row 3: Ch 3, 2tr into next dc, *1dc into centre of shell, 5tr into next dc, rep from * to last st, 3tr into 1-ch, turn.

Rows 2 and 3 make the shell patt. Rep these 2 rows for 4 more rows, then rep row 2; fasten off.

Row 13: Join col B and rep row 3, fasten off.

Long-length cuffs (make 2)

Using col B and 3.5 mm hook, ch 45, turn.

Work as for rows 1–3 of short-length cuffs.

Rep rows 2 and 3 for 13 more times, then rep row 2, fasten off.

Edging (for right-hand cuff)

Using 3.5 mm hook, join col C to bottom of cuff in third shell sp from left. Surface crochet chains to top with a length of multiples of 4. Ch 3 at end. Into 7th surface ch from hook, work (1tr, 1ch) 3 times, then 1tr. *Sk 3 ch, work (1tr 1ch) 3 times, then 1tr into next ch. Rep from * to last 4ch, sk 3ch, 1tr into last ch, fasten off. For left-hand cuff edging, join col C to cuff in third shell sp from right, then cont as above.

Making up
Fold the cuff in half, bring the side edges RS together. Using a tapestry needle threaded with a length of matching yarn, begin at the bottom edge and stitch along the seam until about 2.5 cm from the top (5 cm from the top for the long cuffs); fasten off the yarn.

Rejoin the yarn to the top edge and use a few small stitches to sew the seam together at the top, to make the gap for the thumb (stitch along the seam for about 2.5 cm, leaving approx. 2.5 cm gap for the thumb for the long cuffs). Repeat with the other cuff.

muffler and earmuffs

This matching collar and earmuffs, sporting a pretty flower motif in two colours, will keep you warm without ruining your hair. The short scarf, or muffler, links around the neck to keep out the chill, while the large motifs are attached to bought earmuffs to match.

Muffler

Using col A and 4.5 mm hook, ch 25, turn.

Row 1: 1htr in 3rd ch from hook, htr to end (24 sts), turn.

Row 2: Ch 2 (counts as first htr), htr to end, turn.

Rep row 2 for 60 more rows. Now make gap for scarf to slip through:

Next row: Ch 2 (counts as first htr), 10htr (11 sts), turn.

Cont working in htr on these 11 sts for 19 more rows, fasten off.

Rejoin yarn to outside edge of other unworked side of muffler.

Next row: Ch 2 (counts as first htr), 10htr (11 sts), turn.

Cont working in htr on these 11 sts for 19 more rows, turn.

Next row: Ch 2, 10htr, ch 2 to cross gap, then work 11 htr into other side of muffler, turn.

Cont working in htr across the width of the muffler for 5 more rows, fasten off.

Motif for ends of muffler (make 2)

Using col B and 4.5 mm hook, ch 6, join with sl st to first ch to make a ring.

Rnd 1: Ch 2, 11tr into ring, sl st into top of 2-ch (12 sts), fasten off.

Rnd 2: Join in col C, ch 8, sk 2tr, (1tr into next tr, ch 6, sk 2 tr) 3 times, join with sl st to 2nd ch of 8-ch.

Rnd 3: *(1dc, 1htr, 6tr, 1htr, 1dc) into ch lp, sl st into tr, rep from * 3 times more, ending last rep with a sl st to the last sl st of rnd 2, fasten off.

Rnd 4: Join in col B, ch 9, (htr to next sl st, ch 8) 3 times, sl st to first ch of 9-ch.

Rnd 5: *(1dc, 1htr, 8tr, 1htr, 1dc) into ch lp, sl st into htr, rep from * 3 times more, ending last rep with a sl st to the last sl st of rnd 4, fasten off.

Rnd 6: Join in col C, ch 12, (htr to sl st, ch 10) 3 times, sl st to 2nd ch of 12-ch.

Rnd 7: Ch 5, sk 2 ch, dc into next ch, *ch 3, sk 2 ch, dc into next ch, rep from * to end, finishing with a sl st into each of first and second ch of 5-ch (14 ch lps).

Rnd 8: *Ch 4, 1dc into next ch lp, rep from * to end, sl st into each of 2nd and 3rd ch of first ch lp.

Rnd 9: *Ch 5, 1dc into next ch lp, rep from * to end, sl st into each of 2nd and 3rd ch of first ch lp.

Rnd 10: *Ch 6, 1 dc into next ch lp, rep from * to end, sl st into each of 2nd and 3rd ch of first ch lp, fasten off.

YOU WILL NEED:

- Debbie Bliss Cashmerino Aran, 53% merino, 33% microfibre, 12% cashmere (90 m per 50 g ball), 2 x 50 g balls in Green 502 (col A), 1 x 50 g ball in Pink 602 (col B), 1 x 50 g ball in Orange 615 (col C)
- 4.5 mm hook
- Tapestry needle
- Shop-bought earmuffs
- Fabric glue (optional)

Tension

21 sts and 15 rows over htr = 10 cm.

Finished measurements

Motif: 15 cm diameter.
Muffler: 83 cm long, 11 cm wide.

Rnd 11: Join in col A, *ch 7, 1dc into next ch lp, rep from * to end, sl st into each of 2nd and 3rd ch of first ch lp (14 ch lps).

Rnd 12: *(1dc, 1htr, 6tr, 1htr, 1dc) into first ch lp, sl st to next dc, rep from * to end, fasten off.

Earmuffs (make 2 motifs)

Work as muffler motif to rnd 6, following the colour changes in the same way.

Rnd 7: *(1dc, 3htr, 10tr, 3htr, 1dc) into first ch lp, sl st into htr, rep from * 3 times more, ending last rep with a sl st into 2nd ch of 12-ch.

Rnd 8: Ch 14, (htr to sl st, ch 12) 3 times, sl st to 2nd ch of 14-ch.

Rnd 9: (4tr , 4htr, 1dc) into first ch lp, sl st into 6th ch of ch lp, * (1dc, 4htr, 3tr) into same ch lp, 1tr into htr, (4tr, 4htr, 1dc) into next ch lp, sl st into 6th ch of ch lp, rep from * twice more, (1dc, 4htr, 3tr) tr into last sl st of rnd 8, sl st to first tr, fasten off.

Making up

Using a tapestry needle threaded with a length of col A, sew a motif to each end of the muffler, taking care to conceal the stitches within the work. Sew the motifs to pair of shop-bought earmuffs. Alternatively, attach with fabric glue.

hat and scarf combo

When it comes to keeping out the cold, nothing beats the warmth of the finest merino wool mixed with the softest alpaca. Just looking at these hot colours will warm you up, let alone the extra thickness of the rib pattern, which is guaranteed to ward off any winter blues.

Hat

Using col A and 4.5 mm hook, ch 4. Join with sl st to first ch to form a ring.

Rnd 1: Ch 2 (counts as first htr), 6htr into centre of ring, join with sl st to top of 2-ch (7 sts).

Rnd 2: Ch 2 (counts as first htr), sk first st, 1htr in each st to end, join with sl st to top of 2-ch (7 sts).

Rnd 3: Ch 2 (counts as first htr), sk first st, *1htr in next st, 2htr in next st, rep from * to last st, 1htr, join with sl st to top of 2-ch (10 sts).

Rnd 4: Ch 2 (counts as first htr), 2htr in next st, *1htr in next st, 2htr in next st, rep from * to end, join with sl st to top of 2-ch (15 sts).

Rnd 5: Ch 2 (counts as first htr), *2htr in next st, 1htr in next st rep from * to end of rnd, join with sl st to top of 2-ch (22 sts).

Rnd 6: Ch 2 (counts as first htr), work 2htr into next st, *1htr into next st, 2htr into each of next 2 sts, rep from * to last 2 sts, 1htr into next st, 2htr into next st, join with sl st to top of 2-ch (37 sts).

Rnd 7: Ch 2 (counts as first htr), sk first st, *1htr into each of next 3 sts, 2htr in next st, rep from * to end of rnd, join with sl st to top of 2-ch (46 sts).

Rnd 8: Ch 2 (counts as first htr), sk first st, *1htr into each of next 4 sts, 2htr in next st, rep from * to end of rnd, join with sl st to top of 2-ch (55 sts).

Rnd 9: Ch 2 (counts as first htr), sk first st, *1htr into each of next 5 sts, 2htr in next st, rep from * to end of rnd, join with sl st to top of 2-ch (64 sts).

Rnd 10: Ch 2 (counts as first htr), htr to end of rnd, join with sl st to top of 2-ch (64 sts).

Rnd 11: Ch 2 (counts as first htr), sk first st, *1htr into each of next 6 sts, 2htr in next st, rep from * to end of rnd, join with sl st to top of 2-ch (73 sts).

Rnd 12: Ch 2 (counts as first htr), htr to end of rnd (73 sts).

Rnd 13: Ch 2 (counts as first htr), sk first st, *1htr into each of next 7sts, 2htr in next st, rep from * to end of rnd, join with sl st to top of 2-ch (82 sts).

Rnd 14: Ch 2 (counts as first htr), htr to end of rnd, join with sl st to top of 2-ch (82 sts).

Rnd 15: Ch 2 (counts as first htr), sk first st *1htr into each of next 8 sts, 2htr in next st, rep from * to end of rnd, join with sl st to top of 2-ch (91 sts).

Rnd 16: Ch 2 (counts as first htr), htr to end of rnd, join with sl st to top of 2-ch (91 sts).

YOU WILL NEED:

- Blue Sky DK 50% alpaca 50% merino wool (91 m per 100 g hank), 3 x 100 g ball in Red 2000 (col A), 1 x 100 g ball in Rusty Orange (col B)
- 4.5 mm and 6 mm hooks
- Tapestry needle

Tension
Hat: 6 rows and 7 sts = 5 cm using 4.5 mm hook over htr patt.
Scarf flaps: 6 sts and 4 ribs = 5 cm using 6 mm hook.

Finished measurements
Hat: 66 cm diameter.
Scarf flaps: 77 cm long.

Rnd 17: Ch 2 (counts as first htr), sk first st *1htr into each of next 9 sts, 2htr in next st, rep from * to end of rnd, join with sl st to top of 2-ch (100 sts).

Rnd 18: Ch 2 (counts as first htr), htr to end of rnd, join with sl st to top of 2-ch (100 sts).

Rep the last rnd 6 times more, fasten off.

Flaps (make 2)

Using col A and 6 mm hook, ch 50.

Row 1: 1dc into 3rd ch from hook, dc to end (49 sts), turn.

Row 2: Ch 1 (counts as first dc), sk first st, *1dc into front lp of next st, rep from * to end, working last dc into 1-ch turn.

Row 3: Ch 1 (count as first dc), dc to end turn.

Rep rows 2 & 3 for 4 more times.

Row 12: As row 2, fasten off.

Trim

Join col B to one corner, using 6 mm hook, and work along a side edge.

Row 1: Ch 1 (counts as first dc), then work 9dc across this edge (10 sts), turn.

Row 2: Ch 10, *sk 2 sts, 1dc into next st, ch 10, rep from * to end. Turn.

Row 3: *6dc into loop, 8ch, sl st into 8th ch from hook, turn, 8dc into loop, 1dc into dc, turn, 1dc into each of next 8dc, 6dc into loop. Sl st into dc. Rep from * to end. Fasten off.

Making up

On the edge of the hat, count 13 sts to the left of the centre back (where the yarn is fastened off), mark this point with a piece of contrasting yarn. Take one flap and match the top-right corner to the marked point (the top of the flap is the edge opposite the trimmed edge), then pin the flap to the edge of the hat; sew in place using a tapestry needle and matching thread. Count 13 sts to the right of the centre back and mark this point. Match the top-left corner of the remaining flap to this point, then pin and sew in place as before.

tunisian crochet bag

The Tunisian stitch is almost a combination of knitting and crochet that creates a firm texture and uses a special hook with a knob at one end like a knitting needle.

Using col A and 3 mm Tunisian hook, ch 51, do not turn.

Row 1: Sk 1 ch, *yrh, insert hook in next ch, yrh and draw loop through, yrh and draw through 2 of the loops on the hook, rep from * to end (50 loops on hook), do not turn (this is the first row of Tunisian tr).

Row 2: Yrh and draw through 1 loop, *yrh and draw through next 2 loops, rep from * to end (1 loop remains on hook), do not turn.

Row 3: Ch 1 (counts as first st), sk vertical loop of first st, *yrh, insert hook from right to left under vertical loop of next st, yrh and draw a loop through the st, yrh and draw through 2 of the loops on hook, rep from * to end (50 loops on hook), do not turn.

Row 4: As row 2.

Repeat rows 3 & 4 until 30 rows worked; fasten off.

Making up
Fold the work in half lengthways, RS tog. Using a tapestry needle threaded with matching yarn, sew up the side seams. Turn to RS.

Strap
With RS facing and using 3 mm hook (you can use the Tunisian crochet hook to do conventional crochet), join col A to the top edge of the bag, 2 sts to the right of one of the side seams.

Row 1: Ch 2, 4htr into top of bag so centre st falls on side seam (5 sts), turn.

Row 2: Ch 2 (counts as first htr), 4htr, turn.

Rep row 2 until the strap is the required length, fasten off. Using a tapestry needle threaded with matching yarn, stitch the end of the strap to the other side of the bag, matching the centre of the strap to the side seam.

Motifs
Turn bag upside down. Join col B to 2nd row of Tunisian tr from the bottom fold of the bag, 4 sts in from the right-hand edge. Work between the bars of the sts. Ch 4, into this st sp, work 1dtr, ch 1, 1dtr, ch 1, 1tr. Into next ch sp up, work 1tr, ch 1, 1tr, ch 1, 1dc. Into the horizontal loop of the stitch to left of sp, work 1htr, ch 3, sl st to 3rd ch from hook. Into sp to left of sts just worked into, work 1dc, ch 1, 1tr, ch 1, 1tr, then into st sp below, work 1tr, ch 1, 1dtr, ch 1, 1dtr, ch 1, 1dtr; fasten off. Work motif over 4 Tunisian tr sts at regular intervals over the bag.

YOU WILL NEED:

- House of Hemp Expressions hand-coloured 2-ply hemp (170 m per 50 g ball), 1 x 50 g ball in Mmm (purple) (col A)
- House of Hemp Expressions hand-coloured fine yarn hemp (340 m per 50 g ball), 1 x 50 g ball in Yippi (green) (col B)
- 3 mm Tunisian hook
- Tapestry needle

Tension
Not crucial.

Finished measurements
Approximately 25 cm x 15 cm.

Note
For Tunisian crochet technique, see pages 66–69.

Lacy collar and belt

This lovely lacy-stitch pattern uses the same pattern to make a delicate collar, or in a shorter version it makes a fashionable hipster belt. Use the flower as an oversized button to keep the belt done up. The collar fastens with a ribbon, with or without an additional flower.

YOU WILL NEED:

For the belt:
- Blue Sky Alpaca 4-ply 100% alpaca (100 m per 50 g ball), 2 x 50 g balls in Green 47 (col A), 1 x 50 g ball each in Natural Dark Grey 0012 (col B), and Tarnished Gold 73 (col C)

For the collar:
- Blue Sky Alpaca 4-ply 100% alpaca (100 m per 50 g ball), 1 x 50 g ball each in Fuschia 57 (col D), and Purple 53 (col E)

- 6 mm hook
- Tapestry needle
- 2 m of ribbon
- Needle and sewing thread to match ribbon

Finished measurements
Collar: approximately 98 cm on cast on edge.
Belt: approximately 82 cm on cast on edge.

Belt
Using col A and 6 mm hook, ch 109, turn.

Row 1: 1dc into 2nd ch from hook, *ch 3, sk 3ch, (1tr, ch 5, 1tr) into next ch, ch 3, sk 3ch, 2dc, rep from * to last 8ch, ch 3, sk 3ch, (1tr, ch 5, 1tr) into next ch, ch 3, sk 3ch, 1dc into last ch, turn.

Row 2: Ch 1, *3htr into next 3-ch sp, 1tr into tr, 6tr into next 5-ch sp, 1tr into tr, 3htr into next 3-ch sp, sk 2dc, rep from * to end but work 1dc into last st (instead of sk 2dc), turn.

Row 3: Ch 4, sk 3htr, *1tr into next tr, ch 4, sk 2tr, 1dc into each of next 2tr, ch 4, sk 2tr, 1tr into next tr, sk 6htr; rep from * to end, but finish with sk 3htr, 1dtr into the 1-ch, turn.

Row 4: Ch 5, 1tr into next tr, *ch 3, 1dc into each of next 2dc, ch 3, (1tr, ch 5, 1tr) into next tr, rep from * to end but finish with (1tr, ch 2, 1tr) into top of 4-ch, turn.

Row 5: Ch 3, 2tr into 2-ch sp, *1tr into next tr, 3htr into next 3-ch sp, sk 2dc, 3htr into next 3-ch sp, 1tr into tr, 6tr into next 5-ch sp; rep from * to end but finish with 2tr into next last ch sp, 1tr into 3rd of 5-ch, turn.

Row 6: Ch 1, 1dc into first tr, ch 4, sk 2tr, 1tr into next tr, *sk 6htr, 1tr into next tr, ch 4, sk 2tr, 1dc into each of next 2tr, ch 4, sk 2tr, 1tr into next tr, rep from * to end, finishing with sk 6htr, 1tr into next tr, ch 4, sk 2tr, 1dc into top of 3-ch, turn.

Row 7: 1dc into first dc, *ch 3, (1tr, 5 ch, 1tr) into next tr, 3ch, 1dc into each of next 2dc, rep from * to end, finishing with 1dc into last dc, turn.

Row 8: Rep row 2, fasten off.

Flower button
Using col B and 6 mm hook, ch 55.

Row 1: Work 5tr into every other ch to end, fasten off, turn.

Row 2: Join in col C, ch 1, 6dc, ch 3, sl st into first of ch to make picot, 6dc, ch 3, sl st into first of ch to make picot, 6dc, fasten off.

Making up
The finished flower button will naturally form a spiral – curl this up to make the shape. Thread a tapestry needle with a length of matching yarn and secure the flower shape with a few stitches. Sew the flower onto one end of the belt. Then, when you wear the belt, you can pass the flower through one of the holes in the opposite end to secure it.

Lacy Pattern Collar

Using col D and 6 mm hook, ch 136, turn.

Work rows 1–7, of the belt pattern, then rep rows 2–6, fasten off.

Next row: Join in col E and work one row 7, turn.

Next row: Work one row 2, fasten off.

Making up

Thread ribbon in and out of the gaps on the first row. Thread a needle with matching sewing thread and secure the ribbon with a few stitches. Tie the ribbon together at front with a bow to secure the collar.

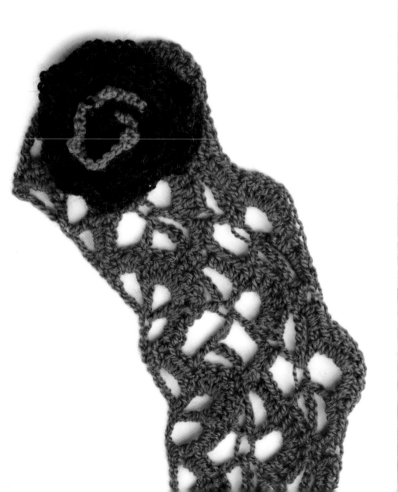

wheels-on-fire slippers

Put your feet up with these fancy slip-ons. The shop-bought insoles will make the bottoms rigid and soft underfoot, and they can be covered with pretty fabric to match. The chart is easy to understand if you follow the tips below.

Pattern notes

When changing to a new colour, change yarn in the stitch before you want the new colour to start. Begin the next stitch in the usual way, but draw the new yarn through the final two loops to finish. The next stitch will be in the new colour. Carry the colour you aren't working with on top of the stitches – the working yarn is worked over it. This is the 'intarsia' method and makes a thicker, carpet-like texture. Loose ends should not 'float' at the back of the work as your feet will catch on them. Work over loose ends to conceal the yarn within the crochet.

Slipper (make 2)

Using a 4 mm hook and col A, ch 4. Join with sl st to first ch to form a ring.

Rnd 1: Ch 1 (counts as first dc), 6dc into centre of ring, join with sl st to top of 1-ch.

Rnd 2: Ch 1, place the yarn marker across the sts from front to back to mark the beg of the rnd, 2dc into sl st, 2dc into rem 5 sts, join with sl st to first dc where marker is placed (12 sts).

Rnd 3: Ch 1, pull out marker from prev rnd and place across sts as before, 1dc into sl st, changing to col B at same time, dc to end, alternating bet col A and B with each st, join with sl st to first dc.

Rnd 4: Ch 1, put marker in place as before, 1dc into sl st, 2dc into next dc, rep 5 times more, foll col chart on page 182, join with sl st to first dc (18 sts).

Rnd 5: As rnd 3.

Rnd 6: Ch 1, put marker in place as before, 1dc into sl st, *1dc, 2dc into next st, 1dc, rep from * to last 2 sts, 1dc, 2dc into next st, join with sl st to first dc (24 sts).

Rnd 7: As rnd 3.

Rnd 8: Ch 1, put marker in place as before, 1dc into sl st, *2dc, 2dc into next st, 1dc, rep from * to last 3 sts, 2dc, 2dc in next st, join with sl st to first dc (30 sts).

Rnd 9: As rnd 3, foll col chart on page 182.

Rnd 10: Ch 1, put marker in place as before, 1dc into sl st, *3dc, 2dc into next st, 1dc, rep from * to last 4 sts, 3dc, 2dc into next st (36 st).

Rnd 11: As rnd 3.

YOU WILL NEED:

- Debbie Bliss Cotton Angora, 80% cotton 20% angora (78 m per 50 g ball), 1 x 50 g ball in Blue 08 (col B), 1 x 50 g ball in Red 11 (col A)
- Short length of a contrasting yarn to use as a marker
- 4 mm and 3 mm hooks
- Shop-bought insoles
- Piece of fabric, approximately 25 x 25 cm, to cover insoles
- Fabric glue

Tension

14 st x 16 rows = 10 cm using 4 mm hook over dc.

Finished measurements

Approximately 24[27] cm long.

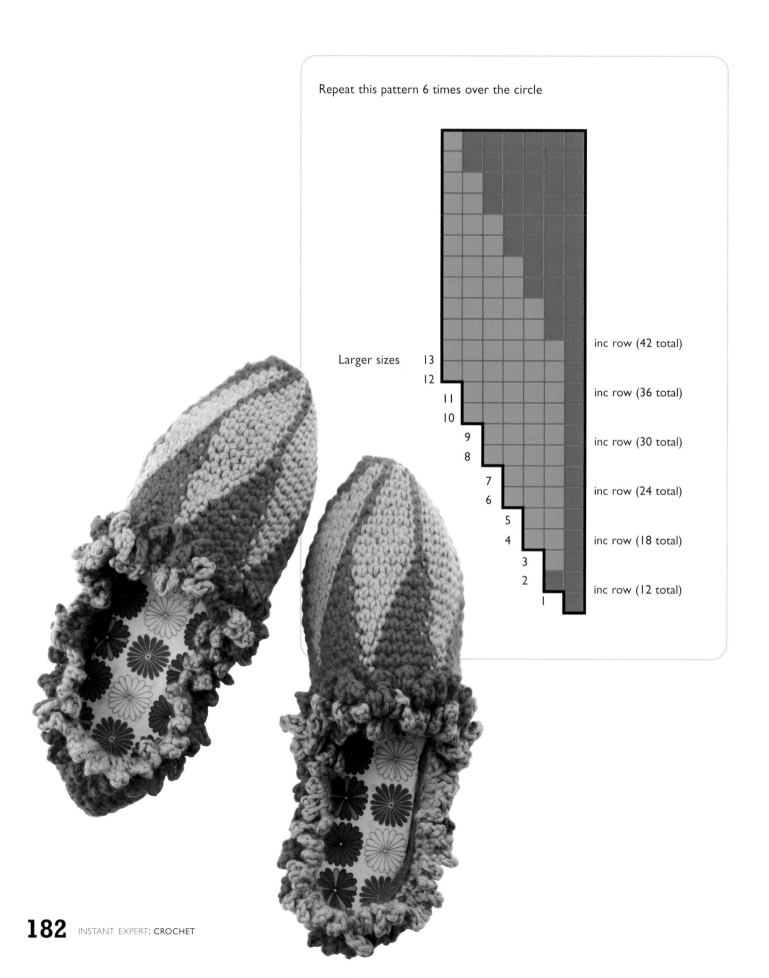

Repeat this pattern 6 times over the circle

Larger sizes

13
12
11
10
9
8
7
6
5
4
3
2
1

inc row (42 total)
inc row (36 total)
inc row (30 total)
inc row (24 total)
inc row (18 total)
inc row (12 total)

Work rnds 12 and 13 for larger size only:

Rnd 12: Ch 1, put marker in place as before, 1dc into sl st, *4dc, 2dc into next st, 1dc, rep from * to last 5 sts, 4dc, 2dc into next st (42 sts).

Rnd 13: As rnd 3.

Foll colour chart opposite, and rep rnd 3 until work measures 11[14] cm.

Sole and sides

After finishing last rnd with a sl st, cont with 2 sl sts into next 2 sts, turn. Cont working in rows as foll:

Row 1: (WS) ch 1 (counts as first dc), 15dc, turn.

Row 2: Ch 1, sk first st, dc to end, working last dc into the 1-ch at edge (16 sts).

Rep row 2 twice [4 more times].

Next (inc) row: Ch 1, dc to end, working 2dc into the 1-ch at edge (18 sts), turn.

Rep row 2 five more times, then rep increase once (20 sts). Rep row 2 until work measures 24[27] cm or required length, fasten off.

Loopy trim

Using 3 mm hook, join col B to the edge of the slipper, at the back seam. With RS facing, work dc all around the edge, fasten off.

Join col A at first dc at back seam, *ch 7, sl st into front lp of next st, rep from * to end, fasten off.

Join col B at first dc at back seam, *ch 7, sl st into back lp of next st, rep from * to end, fasten off.

Making up

Fold the flat part of the slipper in half, RS tog and join by stitching with a tapestry needle threaded with a length of matching yarn or by working dc along the seam (see pages 46–47).

Finishing

To tighten the edge of each slipper and improve the fit, thread a tapestry needle with a long length of col B and weave it in and out of the sts on the dc row of the trim. Try the slippers on and then pull on the loose ends of the yarn to tighten the fit. Tie the ends of the yarn together and remove the slippers. Weave the loose ends into the work.

Place one of the shop-bought insoles on the WS of the fabric and draw round the edge, cut out. Repeat so you have two sole-shaped pieces. Place the insole on the fabric again and draw around it, 3 cm from the edge; cut out. Repeat so you have two slightly larger sole-shaped pieces.

Spread fabric glue on one side of one insole and cover with one of the same-sized pieces of fabric. Repeat with the other insole.

Spread glue on the other side of one insole and cover with one of the larger pieces of fabric, centring the insole on the fabric. Snip into the excess fabric around the edge of the insole, making sure you don't cut into the insole itself. Spread glue around the edge of the insole, to a depth of 3 cm. Fold over the excess fabric, pressing it down onto the glue. Repeat with the other insole. Leave both insoles to dry before placing them in the slippers.

pretty corsages

Make as many of these pretty flowers as you like, varying the colours, pom-poms and buttons to make each one unique. They are a great way of using up all those oddments of wool that are too small to make anything else out of. Have some fun putting together the colours.

Large motif

Using col A and 8 mm hook, ch 4, join with sl st to form ring.

Rnd 1: Ch 1 (counts as first dc), 5dc into ring, join with sl st to top of 1-ch.

Rnd 2: *Ch 7, join with sl st to next st, rep from * to end, finishing with sl st into last sl st of prev rnd (7 ch-lps formed), fasten off.

Make one more in col B.

Small motif

Using col C and 3.5 mm hook ch 5, join with sl st to form ring.

Rnd 1: (Ch 4, 3ttr in ring, ch 4, 1 sl st into ring) 5 times (5 petals formed), fasten off.

Make one more in col D.

Making up

Use the cardboard and col E to make a pom-pom 4 cm in diameter (see page 75). Wash the large motifs in a washing machine on a 40°C cycle or in a very hot hand wash to felt them. Sew the pom-pom to the centre of the col D small motif, then stitch this to the col B large motif. Sew the button into the centre of the col C small motif, then stitch this to the col A large motif. Secure a kilt pin or large safety pin to the back of each corsage with a few firm hand stitches.

YOU WILL NEED:

- Small amount of chunky yarn suitable for felting in pink (col A) and blue (col B)
- Small amount of a DK yarn in pale blue (col C) and pale pink (col D)
- Small amount of a 4-ply in light purple (col E)
- 8 mm and 3.5 mm hooks
- Cardboard (for making pom-pom)
- 2 kilt pins or large safety pins
- Vintage button
- Sewing thread and needle

Tension

Not crucial.

Finished measurements

Approximately 9 cm in diameter.

caring for precious woollens

Having spent so long making your beautiful crochet-wear, it would be a shame to spoil it with careless washing or storage. Fibres are vulnerable when wet and therefore need particularly careful handling in this state.

Washing woollens

Looking after crocheted items is much like caring for your knitwear and depends predominantly on the yarn used. Always wash with care so as not to distort the shape, whatever the yarn. This means using the minimum amount of agitation when it is wet, and drying flat, rather than hanging on a line.

Modern yarns are tried and tested, and many of them can be machine washed, but always check the instructions on the ball band and follow them carefully. Most washing machines have special cycles for woollens and delicates that protect fibres from being weakened by too much friction and heat. As a result, not too much hand-washing is needed any more, although you may prefer this method, certainly for your finer delicates and items made from specialist natural yarns such as alpaca and cashmere.

If you are in any doubt it is best to wash items carefully by hand using gentle soap flakes. Do not leave items to soak. Instead, wash them gently by squeezing and then rinse repeatedly until the water runs clear. Never rub a crocheted garment: wool may felt, and although cotton is tougher, it may 'pill', or bobbles may appear on the surface, if rubbed too aggressively.

Once well rinsed, squeeze out the excess water gently, avoiding wringing or twisting the garment. Then roll the item in a thick clean towel to remove excess water and repeat until you have removed as much water as possible. Alternatively, put the garment in a pillowcase and use the short-spin program on a washing machine.

Most yarns will be colourfast, but if you are not sure, dip a small piece into soapy water and press it on a white cloth. If it leaves a stain, wash it in cold water on its own.

Drying

All hand-made items, whether they are hand- or machine-washed, should be dried flat on either a clean towel or a clothes airer, away from direct heat. If your garment has been distorted, usually by hanging on a hook, the back of a chair or coathanger, try steaming it back into shape with the steam function of your iron.

Storage

Avoid hanging up crocheted garments as this will stretch and pull them out of shape. Instead always fold and put them in a drawer. If you have pure wool items, store them with a moth deterrent such as lavender bags or cedar wood balls.

If you do find moth holes, repair them, if possible, then have the garment dry cleaned or put it in a plastic bag in the freezer for 24 hours. Both these methods should kill any moth larvae. Clean the storage area thoroughly and put moth deterrent in. Try storing woollens in sealed bags when they are not being used regularly.

acknowledgements

The makers

Thank you to all the makers and designers on the following projects:

Carol Chambers
Red cabled suit, peace pink alpaca shawl

Bee Clinch
Pretty corsages, wheels-on-fire slippers, floral dress, boudoir coathangers

Roz Esposito
Pixie hat and scarf, baby play-mat

Susie Johns
Magic shopping bag, rag-rug bath mat, cot blanket, textured cushions, crochet dolls, linen sheet edging

Ruth Maddock
Hooded jacket, all-in-one shrug, curtain tieback, crossover cardigan, chevron skirt, lacy blue camisole

Claire Montgomerie
Cuffs, snow bonnet, leafy muffler, lacy collar, hat and scarf, Tunisian handbag, table centrepiece, trinket boxes, photograph album

Thanks also to Claire Montgomerie for the steps and use of her lovely hands in the step photography. Thank you to **Maia**, **Susannah** and **Charlie** our peerless models. Thanks to **Nina** at Clover for sending us hooks at the eleventh hour, **Robbyn** at Purlescence for the lovely crochet accessories, and **Sheila Williams** our knitting and crochet historian. **Caroline Smith** for casting her eyes over the patterns, and last but not leasst, **Lizzie** and **Viv** for the kind use of their home and studio, and for yet more lovely photography.

Suppliers

Blue Sky Alpacas, Inc.
Luxurious alpacas and organic cotton yarns.
PO Box 387, St Francis,
MN 55070, USA
Tel: 001 888-460-8862
Fax: 001 763-753-3345
info@blueskyalpacas.com
www.blueskyalpacas.com

Clover Euro GmbH
Wooden hooks and supplies
Kontor 4 EG, Högerdamm 39
20097 Hamburg, Germany
Tel: +49 (0)-40-219065-0
Fax: +49 (0)-40-219065-29
info@clovereuro.de
http://www.clover-euro.de

Coats Crafts UK
Patons yarns, Coats crochet cottons and Anchor yarns.
PO Box 22, Lingfield House,
Lingfield Point, McMullen Road,
Darlington, County Durham,
DL1 1YQ, United Kingdom
consumer.ccuk@coats.com
www.coatscrafts.co.uk

The House of Hemp
Beautifully dyed range of hemps on the internet.
Beeston Farm,
Marhamchurch, Cornwall,
EX23 0ET, United Kingdom
Tel: + 44 (0)1288 381 638
tj@thehouseofhemp.co.uk
www.thehouseofhemp.co.uk

Designer Yarns Ltd.
Beautiful Debbie Bliss and Noro yarns, amongst others.
Unit 8-10 Newbridge Industrial Estate
Pitt Street, Keighley, West Yorkshire,
BD21 4PQ, United Kingdom
Tel: + 44 (0)1535 664222
Fax: + 44 (0)1535 664333
jane@designeryarns.uk.com
www.designeryarns.uk.com

Purlescence
Beautiful accessories and bags online
31 Hexham Gardens,
Isleworth, Middlesex,
TW7 5JR, United Kingdom
Fax: +44 (0)870 7059924
sales@purlescence.co.uk
www.purlescence.com

Rowan Yarns
Green Lane Mill,
Holmfirth, HD9 2DX,
United Kingdom
Tel: +44 (0)1484 681881
Fax: +44 (0)1484 687920
www.knitrowan.com

crochet abbreviations

Looking at a crochet pattern for the first time must feel like reading another language. The shortened words are really there to prevent laborious repetition, and of course, to make the patterns shorter and easier to follow. Special abbreviations that are used are mentioned on each pattern page, but these are the main ones that you will encounter.

[ ]	work instructions within brackets as many times as directed.
( )	work instructions within parentheses as many times as directed.
*	repeat the instructions following the single asterisk as directed.
* *	repeat instructions between asterisks as many times as directed or repeat from a given set of instructions.
alt	alternate
approx	approximately
beg	begin/beginning
bet	between
bo	bobble
CC	contrasting color
ch	chain stitch
ch-	refers to chain or space previously made: e.g., ch-1 space
ch-sp	chain space
CL	cluster
cm	centimetre(s)
cont	continue
dc	double crochet
dc2tog	double crochet 2 stitches together
dc3tog	double crochet 3 stitches together

dec	decrease/decreases/decreasing
dtr	double treble
foll	follow/follows/following
g	gram
htr	half treble crochet
htr2tog	half treble crochet 2 stitches together
inc	increase/increases/increasing
lp(s)	loop(s)
m	metre(s)
MC	main colour
mm	millimeter(s)
p	picot
patt(s)	pattern(s)
pc	popcorn
pm	place marker
prev	previous
rb	raised back
rbdc	raised back double crochet (1dc round back of stem)
rbdtr	raised back double treble crochet (1dtr round back of stem)
rbtr	raised back treble crochet (1tr round back of stem)
rem	remain/remaining
rep	repeat(s)

rf	raised front
rfdc	raised front double crochet (1dc round front of stem)
rfdtr	raised front double treble crochet (1dtr round front of stem)
rftr	raise front treble crochet (1tr round front of stem)
rnd(s)	round(s)
RS	right side
sk	skip
sl st	slip sitich
sp(s)	space(s)
st(s)	stitch(es)
tch or t-ch	turning chain
tbl	through back loop
tog	together
tr	treble crochet
trtr	triple treble crochet
WS	wrong side
yd(s)	yard(s)
yo	yarn over
yoh	yarn over hook
yrh	yarn round hook

conversion charts

In an ideal world we would all be using the same measurements. However, for those using old-fashioned or American hooks or yarns, these charts can be used to convert them into metric measurements or commonly used UK terms. If in doubt stick to the metric sizes as these are more accurate. This book uses UK terms throughout.

Hook Conversions

US	Metric
B–1	2.25 mm
C–2	2.75 mm
D–3	3.25 mm
E–4	3.5 mm
F–5	3.75 mm
G–6	4 mm
7	4.5 mm
H–8	5 mm
I–9	5.5
J–10	6
K–101/2	7
L–11	8 mm
M/N–13	9 mm
N/P–15	10 mm
P/Q	15 mm
Q	16 mm
S	19 mm

US/UK Crochet Terms

US	UK	
ss	sl st	(slip stitch)
ch	ch	(chain)
sc (single crochet)	dc	(double crochet)
dc (double crochet)	tr	(treble)
tr (treble)	dtr	(double treble
dtr (double treble)	tr tr	(triple treble)

US/UK Yarns

US	UK
Fingering	4-ply
Sport	Double knit (DK)
Worsted	Aran
Bulky	Chunky

index